Power Skills That Lead
to Exceptional Performance

Power Skills That Lead
to Exceptional Performance

Neal Whitten

BUSINESS EXPERT PRESS

Leader in applied, concise business books

Power Skills That Lead to Exceptional Performance

Copyright © Business Expert Press, LLC, 2024

Cover design by Bob Berry

Interior design by Exeter Premedia Services Private Ltd., Chennai, India

First published in 2023 by
Business Expert Press, LLC
222 East 46th Street, New York, NY 10017
www.businessexpertpress.com

ISBN-13: 978-1-63742-498-8 (paperback)
ISBN-13: 978-1-63742-499-5 (e-book)

Business Expert Press Portfolio and Project Management Collection

First edition: 2023

10 9 8 7 6 5 4 3 2 1

To Barbara, my wingwoman.

Description

This book is for leaders, those who aspire to be leaders, and all employees who desire to take their performance to a higher level.

Do you have the Power Skills needed to achieve the level of success you desire? Power Skills are a top asset in today's ever-changing workplace. This book reveals Power Skills that promote how to think and act accountably for success.

But this book does far more. It describes Power Skills that, if taught and nurtured to *all* employees of an organization or company, will result in the organization continuously and holistically evolving. Adopting these Power Skills can lead to *exceptional performance* both for individuals and for their organizations.

Power Skills discussed include *break the rules occasionally, never avoid necessary confrontation, think for yourself, manage daily to your top three priorities, routinely practice boldness and courage, decide who you choose to be, be a good actor,* and so much more.

The Power Skills include those that are foundational, for team building, and for interacting with your leaders.

An organization should invest in a core set of Power Skills that will form a foundation of its culture and values.

I welcome you to come along for a potentially transformative and game-changing ride in your personal pursuit of the adventure called life.

Keywords

Power Skills; soft skills; exceptional performance; project leadership; leadership traits; team building; employee development; foundational power skills; shared values; team skills; project manager characteristics; how to think; how to act accountably; higher performance; increasing personal effectiveness; people skills; practicing integrity; improve personal value; leader

Contents

Testimonials

"Having enjoyed several of your in-person workshops and other publications over these past twenty years, it's clear that you've done a wonderful job of distilling a lifetime of knowledge down to the concepts expressed in this book. This insightful and pragmatic compendium of Power Skills, *growth exercises, and helpful Q&A is a must-read for any aspiring or well-seasoned leader."*
—**Michael Woore, PMP, Vice President, Information Technology, KSL Resorts**

"Overall, this book is an excellent tool for all project managers at any level and applicable in both business and personal life. It's a new, relevant resource for aspiring PMs as well as a refresher tool for seasoned veterans. I believe this book should also be included in the 'self-help' category as it promotes self-care, self-improvement, and self-empowerment. If you don't take care of yourself first, how do you expect to take care of others?"—**Melani Nierras-Lee, Engineering Services Program Manager**

"Neal Whitten's Power Skills *contains many aha moments of sudden insight and clarity. Whether you are a novice employee or an experienced leader, following the skills prescribed will get you to the next level of exceptional performance, both personally and professionally. It is a book that you will read again and again as different skills resonate more loudly during different times in your career and life."*—**Jennifer Tompkins, Security Manager**

"A must read if you care about your personal effectiveness and seek long-term happiness with your career achievements. Neal teaches you how to grow your personal value and team contribution with this no-nonsense guide to eliminating excuses and increasing personal effectiveness. It's all about how to create and improve the value you bring to the table.... follow the principles and make a lasting difference."—**Tom Conway, IBM Vice President and Toshiba Sr. Vice President (Retired)**

"I have had great success with actionable advice from Neal Whitten. The Power Skills that Neal teaches have been incredibly effective in my professional and personal life. I highly recommend to anyone who wishes to increase their performance!"—**Julie Griffin, Client Success Manager, Financial Services and Software**

"This is such a powerful book for new and also very experienced leaders! It is full of time-tested wisdom and practical, apply-it-right-now skills that people and organizations of all types need to help them deliver better results."
—**Cory Bouck, Asia/Pacific Regional Business Director, Johnsonville Sausage, and author of *The Lens of Leadership: Being the Leader Others WANT to Follow***

Online Courses by Neal and Velociteach®

Neal has authored online courses that address the hottest topics in the workplace and on projects. In collaboration with InSite® by Velociteach (www.velociteach.com), a leader in project management training, Neal brings you 20 self-paced courses in a cutting-edge mobile-learning environment. Earn professional development units (PDUs) and take your career to the next level.

Neal's online courses include:

- 17 Top Reasons Why Projects Fail and What You Can Do to Avoid Failure
- Achieving the Elusive Work-Life Balance
- Dealing With Difficult People: 25 Tips to Stay in Control
- 25 Actions to Build Your Self-Confidence
- Top 10 Mistakes in Conducting Lessons Learned
- Effective Time Management to Getting More Done Every Day
- Escalate Is Not a Dirty Word
- Crash Course in Agile Scrum
- Drive Innovation With Disruptive Thinking

Courses on InSite are fun, convenient, and information-filled and can be taken whenever and wherever you are. These courses are essential in helping you become the very best you can be—whether it's about developing your leadership and professional skills, personal skills or achieving the elusive work-life balance. Save by subscribing to the PDU Passport (www.velociteach.com/browse-courses/pdu-passport/) and gain an all-access pass to every PDU course on InSite, including all of Neal's courses.

Velociteach has offered Neal's readers 15 percent off his InSite courses using promo code **NEAL15** at checkout. Browse courses on InSite at www.velociteach.com/browse-courses/.

Acknowledgments

I would like to thank the following people for their feedback and support through their reviews of the manuscript: Cory Bouck, Jennifer Tompkins, Melani Nierras-Lee, Michael Woore, Barbara Whitten, Tim Kloppenborg, and Kam Jugdev.

I would also like to acknowledge that one of my earlier books, *Neal Whitten's No-Nonsense Advice for Successful Projects*, contained several pieces of information that I carried into this book and expanded upon. The book was published by Management Concepts in 2005 and is now owned by Berrett-Koehler. The information is related to the following topics:

- Mind your own business
- Inspect what you expect
- Seventeen behaviors to master when dealing with your leaders.

And finally, I am grateful to the highly professional staff at Business Expert Press and Exeter Premedia Services Private Ltd. 😊

Introduction

Target Audiences

The target audiences for this book are:

1. Leaders or those who aspire to be leaders. Examples of leaders are project managers and team leaders, managers, executives, and any other leadership positions in a company, institution, or government. This also includes independent entrepreneurs.
2. All employees who desire to take their performance to a higher level. The Power Skills presented can benefit all employees in becoming more productive, accountable, and valuable contributors to their organizations and companies.

What This Book Is About

This book is all about *you*. Do you have the Power Skills needed to achieve the level of success you desire? What do I mean by Power Skills? Power Skills are called by many names such as essential soft skills, people skills, behavioral skills, and personality traits—to name a few. More recently, the term Power Skills has been gaining traction. I like this term the best because these skills allow you to harness the power of your inner self to make things happen at work and in your personal life. Power Skills are not just nice to have; they are a top asset in today's ever-changing work-place. Power Skills are the skills of success.

We all have great potential to achieve things that are most important to us. But my experience is that most of us fall far short from being the best we can be because we don't know how to take accountability and think and act effectively. *This book reveals how to do just that!*

But this book does far more. It describes Power Skills that, if taught to *all* employees of an organization or company—and those employees are steadfastly encouraged and nurtured to implement these Power Skills—will help your organization grow and prosper. Your organization will evolve holistically and continuously make any necessary self-corrections along the way with minimal dependency on management. The most needed changes in an organization will originate and be placed into practice from the bottom up—not the other way through top-down management as it is poorly attempted today in most organizations and companies.

Virtually, all areas within an organization can benefit from the institutionalization of these Power Skills. Adopting these Power Skills can lead to *exceptional performance* both for individuals and for their organizations.

What Does Exceptional Performance Look Like?

Picture this: If all the employees of an organization knew what was expected of them in their jobs and they were trained in the Power Skills necessary to execute on those expectations, the organization would be a formidable force in whatever industry it serves. Yet, most organizations and companies are far from being formidable forces; in fact, most companies are stalled and seem to be doing all they can just to survive.

Example

Let's look at an example of exceptional performance by a leader. We have a new hypothetical company made up of 25 employees. All the employees have been trained in the Power Skills I am talking about—the Power Skills presented in this book. Of course, they also are proficient in their respective technical skills, but this book is about the Power Skills which can be equally important and, depending on your vocation, could be more important than the hard skills.

5 Project Teams; 5 Products

The 25 employees are divided into five project teams of five members each. Each team is building a different product and is led by a different project manager. However, the five products must be integrated and work seamlessly with one another. This is the first time in the company's short history that products must work with one another.

Maria, a project manager of one of the teams, recognizes very early on that her product cannot be successful unless it works perfectly with the other four products. So, what does she do? Maria calls a meeting with the other four project managers and presents the need to architect their products to work with one another.

Creation of Architecture Review Board

They create an *Architecture Review Board* with one technical member from each of the five project teams. This board is responsible to ensure that the interfaces across the products are defined and designed to work as required. They create a design document that describes these interfaces. They also review and resolve any issues that may arise with these interfaces. With this in place, the five teams are off to the races building their products.

Self-Perpetual Growth

What just happened? A major process was just created and put in place without management intervention. Any funding and personnel issues may require approval from management, but otherwise, the organization evolved the needed processes without being told to and without going to management and dumping the issue on them.

Maria, the project manager who initiated creating the Architecture Review Board, did not do so because she was told. Nor did she do it because she wanted more responsibility or wanted the visibility of resolving an issue that affected the full organization. She did so because she had to do her job of building a product that satisfactorily integrates with the other four products. She did so naturally because she was trained to think and act on issues in a responsible manner—to practice self-reliance appropriately. Maria exemplified exceptional performance.

Step back and look at the bigger picture. This fast-growing company of 25 employees will continue to grow holistically and efficiently because each employee knows what's expected of them and has been trained to think and act accordingly by way of the Power Skills that they have adopted.

Power Skill Examples

There are several Power Skills that Maria put in play here:

- *Think for yourself*
- *Mind your own business first*
- *Think like a leader*
- *Routinely practice boldness and courage*
- *Understand and practice empowerment.*

These Power Skills, and others, are described in the upcoming chapters. Also, there will be many more examples of exceptional performance throughout the book.

Dependency on Management Is Too High

Today, for most organizations and companies, as they expand in size and complexity, it is notoriously common for:

- Individuals to become more dependent on their bosses and co-workers for direction
- Individuals to increasingly become more uncertain about the responsibilities or actions expected of them while working on their assignments
- Processes to become entangled in excessive bureaucracy
- Individuals to increasingly believe that they don't matter and that one person cannot make a significant difference
- Individuals to lack effective leadership training.

This situation is the opposite of what should be happening.

My view is that most companies are top heavy with too many managers, both low level and senior managers. We need to place more responsibility and accountability onto the nonmanager ranks. The parent-to-child relationship that often permeates across an organization between management and nonmanagement is not an efficient method of leading—and frankly, no one wants it this way.

With higher expectations placed on nonmanagement, and considerable authority transferred to nonmanagers, I assert organizations will grow holistically and become far more efficient, morale will increase, products and services will improve, and likely employee attrition will slow.

Power Skills

This book is all about those Power Skills that all employees—leaders and non-leaders alike—need to embrace to perform at their best, thus causing their organizations to also perform at their best. You will likely recognize each of the Power Skills I will introduce. However, I have found that most people do not effectively execute these skills. Why? Either because no one made them acutely aware of their importance for them and their company to perform at their best, or because many of these skills are not so easy to implement—though I assert anyone can learn to do so with sufficient practice.

Power Skills give you the real power to get your job done effectively and efficiently. It places the accountability for your actions squarely on you. And you know what? Most people would rather have the authority and accountability that these Power Skills support. When you unleash this power in the nonmanagement ranks, your organization and company will prosper like never before.

24 Foundational Power Skills

The upcoming five chapters describe 24 foundational Power Skills. The 24 Power Skills represent the minimum list of the most important Power Skills based on my experience and observations.

I chose Power Skills that universally apply to everyone, no matter their vocation or job. These Power Skills include a range of actions that can substantially affect a person's performance and effectiveness. I find that it's not enough to only focus on the so-called standard behaviors—as important as they are—such as *understanding and practicing empowerment, embracing integrity,* and *treating others as you would like to be treated.*

Many other Power Skills can also play a critical role in determining a person's performance. Therefore, I have included Power Skills that may not be commonly talked about such as *break the rules occasionally, never avoid necessary confrontation, decide who you choose to be, live in your present moments,* and *be a good actor.*

I find that these 24 Power Skills offer a good balance and help lay a solid foundation for your journey. By the way, you might have a favorite Power Skill outside of the 24 that I have identified. It may very well be a key skill for you to continue to embrace.

Some Power Skills can be difficult to practice and master, depending on the person and the Power Skills in question. For some people, it may take months to truly master some Power Skills, but they are essential for a person to become the best version of themselves and for the organization to be the best it can be. The sooner the members of an organization are taught these Power Skills and put them into practice, the sooner the employees and organization can benefit.

Investment in a Core Set of Power Skills

An organization must invest in Power Skills development across all employees. The best time to initiate this is during the onboarding of new employees. However, existing employees also must all be trained. These Power Skills are so valuable to adopt that I assert successfully acquiring them can enrich anyone's resume and help increase their wages.

An organization should settle on a core set of Power Skills that will form a foundation of its culture and values. These Power Skills are tailored to best meet the needs of the organization. They will become mandatory to ensure everyone is on the same page and knows what is expected of them.

When these Power Skills are first identified, expect many different and sometimes conflicting views among members of the organization. A healthy exchange of views, if refereed by an expert moderator and coach, will help to bond members of the organization closer. The Power Skills that are adopted reflect how each member of the organization will act and interact with others.

Stories Throughout the Book

There are stories throughout this book that show you how you can adopt many of the Power Skills. Admittedly, these Power Skills will stretch you, perhaps uncomfortably in the beginning; but with practice and increasing success, your confidence and drive will flourish. The saying *dare to be great* is a mantra I would like you to keep in mind. Everyone reading this book has the potential to become a star performer—an *exceptional* performer—if they are not already.

What's in It for You?

This book can dramatically benefit both your career and your life. It doubles as a mentor to help guide you through your journey. I welcome you to come along for a potentially transformative and game-changing ride in your personal pursuit of the adventure called life.

Free Takeaways

I have created a landing on my website that contains many takeaways from the upcoming chapters and appendices in useful and printable formats. You will be informed in each chapter and appendix when a takeaway can be printed from my website. I will then direct you to the designated page on my website:

nealwhittengroup.com/powerskills/

Once there, you are free to print any information that benefits you. You are also free to make multiple copies of these takeaways as long as you acknowledge their copyright and do not make them available for sale. These takeaways identify this book and state that they are copyrighted. You can use the material in its existing form.

My intent is to offer this free service for years; however, there is no guarantee it will be available forever. Enjoy!

Let's get to it with the first section.

SECTION 1

Foundational Power Skills

Every day we are faced with challenges. How we meet those challenges determines the success we have throughout our lives. In the next five chapters, I will reveal 24 of the most important leading-edge, best-practice, results-oriented Power Skills that will promote your professional and personal success.

I call these *foundational Power Skills*. You can call upon these skills to help you through nearly any situation or event. These Power Skills can dramatically benefit both your career and your life. This assertion is not an overreach. These Power Skills can easily raise your game in life. Judge for yourself as you move through the book.

Think of each of the Power Skills as a piece of a large puzzle. The more pieces you comprehend and apply, the better you can understand the bigger picture of how to make things happen in the most efficient and effective manner.

As I said earlier, I assert that if everyone in an organization knew what was expected of them and rose to the occasion, they would be a formidable group that grows stronger day to day and week to week. They would become the best of the best. Your personal limitations at work and across your life are directly affected by your willingness and tenacity to deliberately embrace and execute on these Power Skills.

Many of my examples are of projects and teams because most people work within these groups.

I have divided the 24 foundational Power Skills into five categories to enhance their understanding and benefit:

- Be your own bold self
- Take care of current business
- Be a role model by your leadership
- Use constructive interactions to improve
- Be your best whole person.

The Power Skills are listed in no particular order. Each is important at the moment you need to embrace it to accomplish a task, deal with an issue, or create a proper mindset. Each has an example. Some have Q and As at their end.

Let's get into this!

CHAPTER 1

Be Your Own Bold Self

This category reveals the first 5 of the 24 foundational Power Skills:

1. Break the rules occasionally
2. Never avoid necessary confrontation
3. Routinely practice boldness and courage to be a consistently effective leader
4. Think for yourself
5. Do not allow what others think about you to be more important than what you think about yourself.

1.   Break the Rules Occasionally

The first foundational Power Skill is to break the rules occasionally—which is what top performers do. Pat McCarty, retired senior project executive IBM, said,

> *Workplace rules are made for 95 percent of employees 95 percent of the time.*

Pat was not talking about breaking ethical or legal rules. She was talking about taking some risks—going outside the norm—pushing the envelope. If you would like to achieve exceptional performance, then you must think like an exceptional performer.

Oftentimes, you will find that following conventional rules will not effectively or efficiently resolve an issue. Although few so-called rules are written within an organization, many rules are perceived, and it's the perceived rules that often cause members to limit their effectiveness. You want to earn the reputation of thinking out of the box—of being creative in solving issues. I have found that, in most cases, it is *better to beg forgiveness than to ask permission*—providing, of course, that your actions are legal and ethical.

Colin Powell, an American politician, statesman, diplomat, and high-ranking United States Army officer, said,

Being responsible sometimes means pissing people off.

He went on to say,

If you are not pissing someone off occasionally then you are not doing your job.

Of course, Powell didn't mean that it is your job to *pxxx off* people; it's your job to get results.

Example

Let's look at an example of breaking the so-called rules.

Many years ago, I worked for a large company and was the manager leading an organization of about 80 people. We were building a new state-of-the-art software product and were working an 18-month plan. Three months had gone by. This Monday morning, when I arrived at work, there was a voicemail message for me. It was Cedric, a first-level manager in another area of this very large organization. Cedric had assigned three people from his department to write the publications that would accompany the new product. These three people were committed to my project and were doing a fine job both writing and working with my team.

I should add that the larger organization Cedric and I worked within of about 10,000 employees was going through major growing pains. There were phenomenal opportunities to build new software and hardware products for new computer systems that were being released. There were shortages of skilled people to meet the demand.

Voicemail From Cedric

Back to the voicemail from Cedric. Cedric said that the larger organization was growing so fast and the demands for his writers were so high that he no longer had enough writers to meet their needs. Consequently, he was removing the three writers assigned to my project and distributing them across other projects.

On my call back to Cedric, I reminded him that he had committed the writers to my project for its duration. He said that it was out of his control—that these were the pains of success and that there was nothing more he could do. I said *You choose to do nothing*. I said that if he insisted on this path I would escalate the issue to his manager, Wally. He said go ahead. I did.

Escalation to Wally, Second-Level Manager

Again, I got nowhere. Wally repeated the *pains of success* schtick, and said there was nothing he could do, and was unwilling to budge. Again, I said he chose to do nothing and that I would escalate to his boss, Debi, a director who oversees about 300 writers. I had worked for Debi at one time and respected her managerial effectiveness.

Escalation to Debi, Director

Debi also was unwilling to budge and said these are the *pains of success*. Now I knew where this scapegoat phrase had come from. I reminded Debi, as I did the prior two managers that they made a commitment to me. And besides, I did not have the authority to go outside the company and hire writers; I had to go through Debi's organization. You guessed it. Debi didn't budge.

Escalation to Danica, Division Director

I then escalated to Danica, a division director. Same conversation. Same lame (from my perspective) position.

Escalation to Riggs, Division VP

I'm now standing at the desk of Elyse, the executive assistant to the division vice president, Riggs. Riggs had 2,000 people reporting to him, but I am not in his chain of command. It was the end of the day. I had escalated all the way to Riggs' office in one day. People say you can't do that so fast. Of course, you can if you are determined. People must relieve themselves, go to lunch, walk hallways, and ride elevators. People can be found. 😊

I told Elyse I needed to see Riggs as soon as possible. She said that's impossible, he's left for the day. I said, can I see him tomorrow? Elyse said no, he's out of town. I sneaked a peak at Riggs' calendar and said, *It shows that he is back in his office at 2 p.m. tomorrow.* Elyse said, *But he can't see you, his calendar is full when he returns to his office.*

I now needed some information from Elyse. Information she might not normally disclose but I was able to retrieve from a continued conversation with her: What airport is Riggs flying into when he returns and at what time does his plane land? The answers were the very small airport nearby and 2 p.m.

Surprising Division VP at Airport

The next day, I'm at the airport at 1 p.m., an hour early. Standing in the airport lobby, I'm watching planes through a large window as they come and go. About 2 p.m., a small private jet lands. One person exits. Walking toward me is what looks like an executive—they all tend to look alike, whether male or female. I opened the airport lobby door for him and asked if he was Riggs. He belted, *Yes!* and continued walking impatiently.

Arrogance. I really dislike arrogance. But I'm on a mission. I caught up with him and walked him to his car. I told him I needed his help. He has a group that made a commitment to my project but broke the commitment without an alternative solution. I told Riggs that I was a product manager with the responsibility to make a profit and that I cannot make a profit with behavior like this. I asked him if he will help me make a profit for the company. And can we discuss this in his car as he heads back to the work lab?

Riggs, not so politely, said he did not know me and did not want me in his car. However, he respected my gumption and would give me the first slot on his calendar when he returns to his office. I said his calendar was already full. He said he was a VP; he'll move everyone 30 minutes.

The lab was 15 minutes away. When Riggs arrived in his office, I was sitting there like a bad habit that wouldn't go away. Within 15 minutes, the issue was resolved. The writers were returned. The reasoning Riggs used, which I would have used in his shoes, was that when a manager makes a commitment, it must be fulfilled, or an acceptable alternative is put in place.

Breaking Perceived Rules

In summary, there were several actions I made that broke perceived rules such as instantly escalating from manager to manager and surprising, off company property, a company executive I did not know.

By the way, after the meeting, I immediately went to my boss and told him the story before others could. I assumed he would not have supported my actions had I asked permission. I assumed correctly. I got my hands figuratively slapped.

Question

I would be uncomfortable doing what you did. Moreover, I would be concerned about getting a negative reputation. Comment?

Answer

I didn't say it was easy for me. My style is to come to work every day and act as if I own the company, and that company was defined by my domain of responsibility (more on this concept later). In other words, if my company's survival is at stake, then I will do whatever is necessary to resolve the issue, providing it is legal and ethical. I should add, my team and I delivered the product on time 15 months later, and received noteworthy recognition for making things happen on this critical project. Just saying.

2. Never Avoid Necessary Confrontation

A key difference between a highly effective leader and a wanna-be can be summed up with one word: *conflict*. It's how you deal with conflict.

Never avoid necessary confrontation. Always give problems the sense of urgency and importance they deserve.

Example

Let's compare three project managers. The first is a senior project manager, Anthony, with a highly effective track record of delivering projects on time, within budget, and with the required quality.

The second project manager, Molly, has just graduated from a university with a master's degree in project management and is entering the work force. Molly will likely be quite naïve, as we all are when we start out. She will trade integrity for popularity because she wants to be liked and to fit in. She will believe that problems will solve themselves if you just leave them alone. This is a highly dangerous concept that is destined to fail. Molly also believes that teams can lead themselves. This is a myth. Sure, teams arguably can lead themselves, but you probably won't like where they go. Teams need a designated and responsible leader to give them direction and focus, and hold them accountable.

The third, Carlos, is also a senior project manager, like Anthony. But Carlos has a weak track record in that most of his projects are late, over budget, and with low quality. Carlos is quite cynical and typically blames his problems on others. For example, Carlos believes the primary reason for Anthony's success is because Anthony gets the easier projects, while Carlos is given the more challenging projects. Carlos doesn't give Anthony any credit for his hard-earned skills that he has developed over the years. Carlos also complains that Anthony gets all the easy people to work with, while he gets the more difficult people. Here again, Carlos does not give Anthony any credit for his great Power Skills.

Common Project-Related Problems

All three project managers will have similar project-related problems to deal with such as availability of staffing, acquiring members with the right skills, technology issues, sufficient funding, poor estimates, project-scope creep, working with difficult clients or management, conflicting priorities, and so on. Just because Anthony appears to always be successful with projects does not mean that he is immune from these common problems—no one is.

The key difference between Anthony—an effective project manager (PM)—and the other two project managers is that Anthony likely will confront problems more quickly, with the sense of urgency and importance they deserve, while less-effective PMs may tend to avoid conflict, causing many of these problems to drift. The effective project manager will go after problems before they have a chance to morph into more serious issues.

Anthony never avoids necessary confrontation and will practice the philosophy that problems do not go away unless he takes appropriate action to mitigate them. Less-effective PMs tend to be too soft and less sure of themselves as well as the appropriate action to take. The avoidance of necessary conflict is a hallmark of the less effective. Your continued effectiveness is related to how well you deal with conflict.

You might be wondering if Anthony, in never avoiding necessary conflict, happens to be one of those few folks who actually likes conflict. He isn't and doesn't. But he recognizes that if he runs or cowers from conflict then his success and career will be largely handicapped.

Conflict

Let's pause for a moment and look a bit more into what I mean by conflict. By *conflict*, I mean disagreement or potential collision with another's views or intentions. Facing problems and solving them often require confrontation with another person. My experience is that over 95 percent of conflict is what I call benign. It really is not a big deal, and we make too much of it.

Example

Lillie Kate and Michelle are great friends at work. They will be meeting today to negotiate an issue between them. Lillie Kate has never had to negotiate an issue with Michelle. And Michelle has a reputation of being a tough negotiator—she never seems to lose.

Prior to the meeting, Lillie Kate is feeling rather intimidated and anxious. She has a high aversion to conflict, but she does not want to lose.

As the two of them meet in a designated room to negotiate, one of them shares a humorous story not related to the meeting. The story has the effect of taking some of the tension away from Lillie Kate.

They then both get serious with the negotiations, and before they know it, the negotiations have ended, and the issue is resolved. It's a win–win—which is what all negotiations should strive for. (No one really wins when there is a win–lose.) They go back to being great friends. This scenario represents how most conflict plays out. We almost always expect the worst and it doesn't occur—often nothing even close.

Why Do We Fear Conflict?

Now the question is begged: Why do so many of us fear conflict? Is it a learned condition, or is it inherent in our makeup? Why do we fear that in a confrontational situation someone will yell at us, make us look bad, cause us to lose face and respect? Well, none of these things happen in almost all cases. However, my experience is in less than five percent of confrontational situations, these things do happen, we are yelled at and so on. But this behavior is never acceptable. People who behave this way are what I call professionally immature. By the way, the likelihood is high that all of us have demonstrated professionally immature behavior sometime in our past.

I should add a footnote here, in the remote likelihood that you at all fear for your safety, then avoid the conflict and seek advice, counsel, or other help before engaging with the other person.

Bottom Line on Conflict

Do not be intimidated by others. It is important to be decisive in ensuring that the best business decision is made—even when others may not be happy with your decision.

When you have a conflict to face, almost never consider if you are up to it. Don't talk yourself out of it. Don't question if you have the courage to move forward. Just do it. After a while, dealing with conflict will not be such a big deal. It will become second nature and you will see your effectiveness greatly benefit from this Power Skill.

Question

Why do you say no one really wins if the outcome is win–lose?

Answer

In a win–lose, someone has lost. If the so-called winner has more negotiating to conduct with the so-called loser, it will not go well. The goal should always be win–win, which typically requires some compromise. The best negotiators look for the other party to feel like they have also benefited from the negotiations.

3. Routinely Practice Boldness and Courage

You cannot be a consistently effective leader or reach a high level of performance if you do not demonstrate boldness and courage.

Boldness Defined

What do I mean by boldness? Boldness is the act of responding to a situation in a manner that may be viewed as daring to some but is essential to effectively address the issue at hand. Boldness is all about taking initiative—especially where others may hesitate or withdraw. By boldness, I do not mean being rude, reckless, insensitive, arrogant, or obnoxious. These attributes are never acceptable.

Observe the people around you who are making positive changes in their organizations or projects. Their actions require boldness. After a while, you may not think of these co-workers as bold, but simply as effective leaders. However, boldness is an essential element of all consistently effective leaders.

Boldness Perspective

Picture this: We are observing two people who are identical in their level of knowledge, skills, and experience. Of course, in real life we cannot find two people exactly alike; but for this example, we did, and here they are. But wait, there is one difference: One person has an average level of boldness—which really isn't very much—and the other person is clearly bold. My experience is that the person who consistently demonstrates bold behavior will far outperform the person who does not—not just at work but in their personal life as well.

A behavior of boldness helps propel a person beyond what he or she might otherwise achieve. In fact, boldness has such a profound impact on the effectiveness of one's performance that I find it curious that this trait is not talked about more in the leadership and project management arenas.

Courage Defined

Let's now look at courage. By courage, I simply mean the act of confronting a fear—something that we may be afraid of, but choose to face, nonetheless.

My experience is that the number-one reason why leaders fail is that they are too soft; they have weak backbones. They lack the courage to be as effective as they should and need to be. It's not easy standing up to those around you, be they executives, clients, vendors, contractors, peers, or team members. But if you expect to be consistently successful as a leader or employee, you must demonstrate the courage to lead yourself and your team to success. It's not about effort or lofty intentions; it's about results.

Courage: Fake It!

People will often say to me that they respect leaders who demonstrate courage but that they don't know how to acquire courage for themselves. If you feel you have too little courage, then I suggest you just *fake it!* You read correctly. Fake it! Why? As insincere as this may sound, it's because no one can tell the difference between real courage and fake courage. What's interesting about this approach is that we become what we think about all day long. If you think courageous thoughts and continuously practice courageous behaviors day-to-day and month-to-month, you will become courageous. Courage is only a thought away. As a leader, your job is to demonstrate the courage to lead.

Short Exercise

Place a hand on the top of your head. Move it to the back of your head. Now move it a bit further down to just below the neckline. Rub around. What do you feel? It's a backbone! You have a backbone! Don't be afraid to use it. The more you do, the more it will feel comfortable to do so.

A bit cheesy? Absolutely! But you can *acquire* a backbone just as much as anyone else. I believe in you! I just need you to believe in you, if you don't already.

Quote About Courage

I like the quote by the French-born U.S. writer Anais Nin, who said,

Life shrinks or expands in proportion to one's courage.

Courage plays a big role in how our lives play out.

Question

I want to be bold. I respect boldness in others. I believe my performance would benefit if I could regularly practice boldness. But I am uncomfortable getting attention, particularly if it comes with negative views about my behavior. Comments?

Answer

You must decide who you choose to be. Don't allow others to decide it for you. You can work at becoming bolder if it is important to you. Perhaps a mentor or coach can help you. Maybe a close co-worker. But whatever you do, don't give up on becoming who you choose to be. You will better understand where I am coming from after you have reviewed the 24 foundational Power Skills.

4. Think for Yourself

Learn to challenge tradition, authority, and the status quo in a professional and mature manner. Routinely question your own behaviors and actions.

Most People Don't

Of the billions of people on this planet, my experience is that most of us do not think for ourselves. Oh, we may think that we do think for ourselves, but we blindly follow charismatic show persons—be they talk-show hosts, celebrities, or anyone else in a talking-head position. We allow ourselves often to be mindlessly led. Habit becomes the status quo, and we ignorantly parrot things like, *Well, that's the way we have always thought about it or done it!*

Most Important Lesson

Perhaps the most important lesson to learn from working on projects and within organizations—and from just living life—is to think for yourself. Otherwise, you become hostage to the past with its outdated and ineffective ideas. You become a willing victim of indifference, mediocrity, narrow-mindedness, and unimaginative thinking. You are stuck inside the proverbial box, doomed to repeat past mistakes. Eventually, you and those you lead can become grossly ineffective.

Example

Kiara is a bright, experienced senior manager who unknowingly has a problem thinking for herself. I was conducting a workshop at a client company—a workshop that discussed Power Skills such as those in this book. The senior management was interested in me training hundreds of employees but first chose for me to train the top-level people in the organization so they can both learn and support these concepts throughout the organization. The class had about 40 participants. When working with senior management, I will often put folks on the spot to see how well they understand, practice, and are committed to these concepts.

Kiara was the head of the testing organization made up of about 150 people. These testers were part of a much larger software and web development organization. Kiara told me that she had been in the testing business for over 25 years and considered herself an expert on testing.

Question 1: What Is a Tester's Role?

I said to Kiara: *Let's say that I am the project manager of a project that is building a software product. You are a tester on my project. Tell me what you view your job is as a tester.* Kiara said, in so many words, that her job is to make sure that she understands the product's requirements—that is, what are the problems that we are out to solve with this product. She said that she must also understand the scope and specifications, because they define the product to be built that is intended to satisfy the requirements. She goes on to say that, as a tester, her job is to ensure that the product is built to specifications and that those specs truly do solve the problem defined in the requirements—and the product solves it in an acceptable and easy-to-use manner. I said to Kiara that she did well in defining her job at a high level.

Question 2: Is a Tester Accountable for the Quality Delivered to Production?

I then asked her a second question: *As a tester, are you accountable for the quality of the deliverable to production?* Kiara said, *Absolutely, yes! Nothing gets to production without first being tested by me.* I said, *Good for you: 2 for 2.*

Question 3: Is a Tester Accountable for Quality Delivered to Her?

Kiara incorrectly answered the third question. Most people I ask do. I asked her if she was accountable for the quality of the deliverable she receives from the development organization. She said, *No. I do not own development. They don't work for me. I have no control over them. I accept what they give to me and then ensure that quality is tested into the product before it goes to production.*

Wrong Answer!

I then made the buzzer sound *eeeghttt!*, implying *wrong answer!* I told Kiara she is accountable for the *quality* of the deliverable to her. Of course, the developers are also accountable, but they don't always perform to their responsibilities. I told Kiara that she has all the power she needs to ensure the correct level of quality. She has approval rights on both the requirements and specifications documents. She has approval rights on the process that development uses to build the product. She can attend design reviews and code inspections if she chooses. She also has approval rights on the testing that the development organization must perform before she will take possession of the product for her testing. She has all the power she needs. The problem is she doesn't exercise it. Kiara assumes this is the way to do things because this is how it's been in the organization for years. Kiara is not thinking for herself.

You Are Accountable for the Quality of the Deliverable

If the members of a project want to perform at their best and produce the required quality product, then the project manager needs to hold each project member accountable for the quality of the deliverable to them. This means that the person receiving the deliverable must get out of their proverbial office and have a conversation with the producer of the deliverable to ensure the necessary quality is being delivered. It doesn't matter how things were done yesterday. It matters are we doing them in the best acceptable manner today.

You Are Accountable for the Timeliness of the Deliverable

I want to take this example a bit further. The project manager should also hold each project member accountable for the *timeliness* of the deliverable to them. Here again, a person waiting on a deliverable should infrequently be surprised if it is delivered late, because both parties should be communicating and working closely with each other.

Furthermore, if a deliverable will be late, its harmful impact should be minimized because the two parties negotiated how best to deal with the late delivery, such as having a portion delivered so some work progress can proceed.

Regular and Close Communications

Project members should be held accountable for both the *quality* and the *timeliness* of the deliverables to them. This means, for example, that project members should not primarily rely on routine project tracking meetings for their information; moreover, they should rarely be surprised with new news when they do attend these tracking meetings. Project members should have regular and close communications with the folks who own the deliverables on which they are dependent. This behavior goes against conventional wisdom in most companies. But it also highlights how we often don't think for ourselves.

Question

If I truly do think for myself, that would likely cause me to disagree more with my co-workers. Is that really a net positive?

Answer

Listen to what you just said. You are implying that you should blindly accept the status quo rather than be a source for truth and progress. A team grows stronger and is far more effective when there is healthy debate among members. Of course, you want the discussion to be respectful.

Question

Are you also saying that I should always insist on my way of thinking if I believe that I am in the right?

Answer

Of course not. However, I do expect you to make a compelling case for your point of view. If you do, your position likely will win out in most cases. However, compromise is an important trait of the best leaders, so expect it to be a common part of the landscape.

5.   Do Not Allow What Others Think About You to Be More Important Than What You Think About Yourself

At some time or another, you will find people who disapprove of your behavior or your decisions. You might even project those feelings toward others from time to time. Even the people you love, and who love you, will at times disapprove of your actions.

Just Opinions

Keep in mind that other people's opinions are just that—opinions. If you allow what other people say about you to immobilize you—to impact your thoughts or performance negatively—then you are saying, in effect, that what other people think about you is more important than what you think about yourself. Don't give that power over to another person. Listen for helpful snippets from them but remain in control of you.

Being Liked

How important is being liked to you? Most people want to be liked. My experience is that many people have *being liked* as a primary objective each day they go to work.

I believe that being liked is overrated. I would not recommend going to work with a primary objective of being liked. Why? Because you are going to have many days where you failed in that objective, and you may be greatly disappointed. I suggest instead, when you go to work, have the objective of demonstrating integrity. Simply put, integrity is knowing the difference between right and wrong and choosing the right action. If you routinely demonstrate integrity, you will likely be respected. If you are respected, you likely will be liked. But even then, there are no guarantees. (More on integrity later.)

By the way, I don't place a great need on you liking me. If I did, my messages and their delivery would be different. But I do care about you. It is my objective to touch each and every one of you in some beneficial way so that you notably benefit from reading this book, even if it is only a reinforcement—a reminder—of what you already know and practice.

You may say: *Really? You don't care if we don't like you?* Look, I would love for all of you to love me but it's not going to happen. It could be that in the first 30 minutes of reading, someone says to herself or himself: *Oh my gosh! He reminds me of my Ex!* … and that is not intended to be a compliment! There is nothing I can do about that. Therefore, I do not perpetuate the need to be liked, but I do want to be effective.

Parable

I like the lesson in this parable that perhaps you may have heard.

There was a young cat running around in a circle chasing its tail. It could not quite reach its tail and eventually began to tire. An older, wiser cat looking on asked the young cat what it was doing. It replied that it was told that happiness is in its tail and if it could grab ahold of its tail, it would have eternal happiness. The older cat said, *You have been told correctly, happiness is in your tail. But I have found that if you do not chase your tail, but instead go about fulfilling your dreams, it will follow you everywhere you go.*

Don't chase after the approval of others; do the right thing and it will mostly come to you.

Question

Say what you will, but I do care what people say about me. I don't see me being able to change this feeling in me. Comment?

Answer

Look, we all want to be liked. However, you don't want to depend on being liked to function effectively and successfully. It is achievable to both want to be liked and still maintain control over your thoughts. It's about not giving others the power over your future thoughts and actions. You must remain in control of you if you care about your integrity and independence.

Question

What if I am not liked by a co-worker, yet I view the co-worker has inappropriately judged me from misinformation? Should I attempt to correct this?

Answer

It may be possible to have a private meeting with the co-worker and walk away with increased respect for each other. But it is also possible that the person will hold firm to her or his beliefs. I respect you for trying. However, I want to caution you to not chase after most of these situations. If you do, you are letting it negatively control you. The higher your level at work and the more visible you become, the more frequent you will find yourself in these situations. It's just a simple fact of life that no one can fully avoid.

CHAPTER 2

Take Care of Current Business

This category reveals the next 5 of the 24 foundational Power Skills:

6. Manage daily to your top three priorities
7. Mind your own business first
8. Live in your present moments
9. Don't make it personal or take it personally
10. Embrace integrity in all that you do.

6. Manage Daily to Your Top Three Priorities

My experience is that most leaders—most employees—do not know how to effectively manage their time. While most people start their day with a to-do list, the list is typically picked apart by working on the low-hanging fruit—the easier items, while the more important tasks continue to be deferred—kicking the proverbial can down the road. The list is also quickly abandoned in favor of interruptions, noise, and minutia that come your way.

Put You on the Spot

If I could put you on the spot right now and ask you what are your top three priorities or problems at work (by the way, priorities and problems mean the same thing to me in this context), and you could not rattle them off within three snaps of your fingers, then you are not a consistently effective leader or employee.

You might be thinking how dare I judge you by so little information about you, that if I would just give you a few minutes, you could come up with your top three priorities. But if you need time to identify them, then I restate my assertion that you are not a consistently effective performer. Instead, you are allowing your day to be managed by others, rather than taking charge and managing to the most important priorities. You are too soft if you are not seizing control of your domain of responsibility and primarily managing to your top three priorities each and every day.

Story

I will show you just how important this Power Skill is to your continued success through a story. I am sitting in my office outside of Atlanta, Georgia, USA, and receive a call from a senior vice president—whom I will call Tommy—of a large U.S.-based company. He was calling from his Atlanta office where a portion of his company is located. He had just gotten my name from a major consulting firm that suggested to him I may be able to help him and that I was located nearby.

Big Project, Big Trouble

Tommy said that he had inherited a project six weeks ago because of corporate organizational changes. The project was originally expected to be 11 months in duration and three years had gone by. Furthermore, the project was expected to have peaked at 60 team members, but today the project has over 500 full-time members. Tommy said that he did not know when the project would end.

Tommy asked me if I would come in and turn the project around. I replied, *Absolutely ... NOT*. He asked if that is because I don't know how. I said I do know how and have done this many times. If I took this job on, then I would only have two or three clients a year, and I prefer having dozens of clients a year.

Conduct Project Review

Tommy asked if I would be willing to visit for two days and conduct a project review and tell him where he needs to go from here. That, I said, I would be happy to do. I met with about a dozen people who had hundreds of slides. I asked hundreds of questions. At the end of the two days, I visit Tommy in his office and reveal to him his top five priorities or problems that need to be addressed on the project. Normally, I would focus only on the top three, but because of the size and complexity of this project, I identified five top priorities.

Top Problems Revealed

For starters, I said that the project had essentially been run by executives that change every six months or so. Most executives do not have great project management skills, and even if they did, this project was too large for an executive to take on and also perform his standard duties. I said he needed to identify one person who will own the project—someone who will be held accountable—someone called the project manager.

The next problem was product requirements. Oh, the project had them, but they were never approved and never placed under change control. In fact, they were changing nearly every day.

The third problem was the development process being followed. There were 10 development teams, each operating as silos with different development processes. A few of the development processes were well thought out, but most were sketchy at best. And I identified two more major problems.

Numerous Secondary Problems Were Not Revealed

Tommy asked me if I found any other problems beyond the five. I said I did—75 additional problems. Tommy then asked me to go through the list with him. I said that I would not do that. My fear was that he would start assigning resource to work them off. Tommy said that of course he would begin working them off so that they didn't become so big that they made the top priorities list. I said again that was exactly why I was not sharing them with him. I said, however, that I would share them with the new project manager he would assign. I told Tommy that was precisely why the project was in trouble: *Because no one laser-focused daily on the top three priorities over the past three years; instead the secondary issues continued receiving the primary attention, yet few of those issues were ever satisfactorily closed.*

The Number One Reason Why Projects Get in Trouble

My major assertion: *The number one reason why projects get in trouble is that the project manager does not manage to the project's top three priorities daily.* I have never seen this statement on a list of the top 10 reasons projects fail—*but this is it—the number 1 reason!* We typically see the usual suspects on the top 10 list such as weak product requirements, scope creep, unreliable estimates, incomplete staffing, poor communications, weak senior stakeholder support, and others.

So how did I figure this out—that the number one reason for project failure is that the project manager did not manage to the project's top three priorities daily? I am not the smartest guy, but I am a relatively old guy who has been around the project management industry for a long time. I have conducted over a hundred reviews of projects that were failing. When I do this, I always summarize at the end of the review the top three priorities or problems that the project manager must immediately resolve.

When I step back and look at the top three lists, the ah-ha moment reveals itself. The problems on the top three lists should have been solved not days but weeks or months earlier—and in some cases years earlier depending on the duration of the project. Had the project manager managed to his or her priorities *daily*, these problems would not still be around.

Start Day With Your To-Do List

So, let's talk about how to manage daily to your top three.

You should begin your day with a to-do list. Most people do. You can put the list together at the start of your next workday or, as I do, the evening before that workday when your mind is active from the day and you already have a good sense of what's important to achieve the next day. I also like to know my top three priorities the night before so that my mind can start working them while I am sleeping. Everyone can do this. For example, clearly express the problem you would like solved just before you fall asleep, and when you wake, the problem will not look so difficult, and options will emerge for you to pursue.

By the way, having a to-do list created the night before helps to reduce work-related stress that evening when I am home. My evening becomes much more enjoyable and relaxing.

Focus Primarily on Your Top Three

Let's say your to-do list has 10 items on it: your top three and a bottom seven. Most project managers will likely have more than 10 items on their to-do list, but I want to keep the list to just 10 in this example to better illustrate my points. When your day ends, make sure that you have spent an appropriate amount of time that day working on your top three priorities. Even if you only made significant headway on one of your top three priorities, you should feel good about what you accomplished that day.

If the day ends and your top three were not touched, but you managed to cross off your bottom seven, do not feel good about your accomplishments that day. Why? You worked on the wrong things. Resist the urge to work on lower priority items.

As a handy rule of thumb, if you have 30 minutes or more free time, make sure you are focused on a top three priority. This is key: The value you bring to your project, your organization, and your company—your contributions—is directly proportional to your efficiency to work off your top three priorities, not your bottom seven. Bear with me as I repeat this because it is so important: *The value you bring to your project, your organization, and your company—your contributions—is directly proportional to your efficiency to work off your top three priorities, not your bottom seven.*

Create Mini-Plans

Your top three priorities on your to-do list should be worked off your list typically within two to three days. If occasionally you have top three items on the list for up to a week that's okay. If you see any of the top three items requiring weeks or months to solve—and are not sure how to get them off your list within two to three days—then here's what you do. Let's say one of your top three priorities will take you a month to solve. Then put together a four-week plan. Identify the activities, their dependencies, their durations, and who owns them. Then get agreement from all the people necessary to make the plan whole and fully committed, and track the four-week plan like you do any other plan. That priority is now being taken care of with a committed plan and you can now remove it from your top three lists and add a new one.

Occasionally Working the Top Three Priorities Can Be Elusive

If occasionally you come to work and find that you are not able to work on any of your top three priorities because of that day's fire fights and interruptions, that's okay. You work in a complex, dynamic environment. This happens. However, if it happens routinely, it's not okay. If you cannot routinely work off your top three priorities within two to three days, then you are the problem. If you are not working them off, no one else will—this is your domain of responsibility. You need help and it is up to you to seek and obtain the appropriate help. A tip here is to make sure that you are keenly aware of what your top three priorities are throughout your workday so that you are working them at every appropriate moment.

Repeat: The Number One Reason Why Projects Get in Trouble …

Before we end this topic, I want to restate what my experience has shown to be a fundamental fact: The number one reason why projects fail is *Because the project manager does not manage to his or her top three priorities daily.* Knowing this and appropriately adjusting your behavior can significantly increase the success of your projects—and your career.

Question

Is *manage daily to your top three priorities* your full position on time management?

Answer

Not at all. However, it is an exceptionally important aspect of successful time management. Here are a few other time management snippets to noodle.

- Time management is not about being busy; it's about being effective and getting more done in less time
- A big difference between effective and noneffective people is the things they choose *not* to do

- Before you start a new task, ask yourself if this is the best use of your time
- Learn to accept *good enough*
- Effective time management can significantly and positively affect the rest of your life.

I am reminded of a statement accredited to Eugène Delacroix, a French Romantic artist (1798–1863), *We work, not only to produce but to give value to time.* Many of the Power Skills in this book help you make the best use of your time.

7.   Mind Your Own Business First

Of the broad body of knowledge, skills, and special insights that I have acquired over the years—information that has greatly helped me become a more effective leader and employee—one of the most helpful pieces of information to affect my thinking and behavior is this: *When you go to work each day, behave as if you own the business and that business is defined by your domain of responsibility.*

You Are a Businessperson First

We are all faced with making many dozens—perhaps hundreds—of meaningful decisions a week. If we get in the habit of making these decisions as if we were making them for our own personal business, I assert that we not only would make better decisions overall, but that we would make them more quickly. You are a businessperson first and an employee second. It's all about business.

Focus First on Your Assignment

When you start your work each day, do *not* focus on moving your company forward. If possible, do not focus on your company at all. Yes, you read correctly. Instead, focus first on your assignment as if you have the most important assignment in the company—because you do—to you. If you aren't looking out for your assignment, nobody else will. Channel your energies toward successfully completing your assignments—*your domain of responsibility*. If everyone in your company focused first on his or her domain of responsibility, the company would do just fine. In fact, your company would probably be more successful than it is today.

Domain of Responsibility

Your domain of responsibility includes all responsibilities and commitments that fall within the scope of your assignment. In short, it is the area for which you are accountable. Focusing on your domain of responsibility doesn't mean that you don't care about your company. Your actions demonstrate the opposite. The success of your assignments strengthens the success of your company. Focus on you and your team members being accountable for their respective domains of responsibility and the rest will follow.

Example

You own the company. You have 10 projects going on at any point in time: Project 1 through Project 10. For simplicity, let's say that you also have 10 project managers—one for each project. Project 1, run by Matt, is especially important to you because it is responsible for 30 percent of the revenue next year. The other nine projects are equally weighted in terms of the revenue they bring in next year—about eight percent each. Of course, eight percent revenue is not chump change, but it is hardly as significant as Project 1's 30 percent.

Here is a question for you as the business owner. You plan to have all 10 project managers in a meeting to discuss your expectations of them. What do you tell the nine project managers to do if Matt's project, Project 1, gets in trouble and Matt requests help from one or more of the other nine project managers? Naturally you want to protect the 30 percent revenue you expect from a successful Project 1. Some possible answers might be:

A. Do whatever you need to do to help Matt with Project 1.
B. Help Matt any way you can, providing it does not negatively impact your own schedules and commitments.

C. Do not volunteer to help Matt at all. Require that he first go through a mediator to ensure that Matt's requests are reasonable and are in the best business interests of the company.

D. Require that Matt go first to your manager and then do whatever your manager directs you to do.

E. Other.

When I play out this scenario in a live class, most of the respondents choose A: Do whatever you need to do to help Matt with Project 1. Let's run with this answer for a moment. Let's also fast forward. Matt's project is indeed in trouble. Matt approaches Katie who is the PM for Project 2 and informs her that he needs her help. Matt says that she has Coleman on her team who has skills that he desperately needs. Matt requests Coleman for a three-week period. If Katie gives up Coleman for three weeks, she knows that she no longer can meet her project's commitments. What does she do? What should she do? Well, if you, as the company owner, told her answer A, then Katie sacrifices her project and hands over Coleman for three weeks—or maybe longer. You probably see the problem here. Worst case scenario, Matt may have caused all nine projects to be sacrificed—70 percent of next year's revenue—to save his project that contributes only 30 percent revenue.

Always Find Two Hours

Let's go back to the question of what you should tell your nine PMs to do if Matt needs help from one or more of you. If I were the owner, I would state two directives. The first is, if anyone comes to you, a PM, or to anyone on your team and asks for up to two hours of their time, you always say *yes*. As a professional, you should always be able to find two hours to help someone. The message here that the company owner is sending is that we are a team, and we help each other when we can.

Help Others but Not to the Point That It Harms Your Commitments

As the company owner, the second directive is, when someone asks for your help, you help them to the point you can. However, never voluntarily sacrifice your project for another. As a PM, you do not have the authority to break your commitments; only the senior stakeholders who you made those commitments to have that authority. So, in the case where Matt requests Coleman for three weeks but by reassigning Coleman for that long, Katie can no longer meet her commitments, Katie tells Matt *no*. But she is not snippy about it. She may even say to Matt, *But I am willing to go to the company owner with you if you want the issue resolved there. If the company owner chooses to sacrifice my project, then I can read an org chart—I will do as directed. But I do not have the authority to voluntarily sacrifice my project.*

By the way, in general, I believe in answer B: Help Matt any way you can, providing it does not negatively impact your own schedules and commitments. However, answers C, D, and E can be workable depending on the process that you choose to follow in an organization.

Remember the point of this segment: Mind your own business first. If your domain of responsibility is well looked after, this is the best thing you can do for your company and the business.

Question

I don't think it is so easy to always be able to find two hours to help a co-worker. Doing so could be painful for the person being asked to sacrifice the two hours. Comments?

Answer

Most times, to help a co-worker will take far less than two hours, maybe 5 to 10 minutes. On the less-likely case where it will take up to two hours, depending on the urgency of your assignments, you may occasionally have to pass or put off the help for a short time. However, the message remains that we should strive to help our co-workers in situations requiring two hours or less.

8.   Live in Your Present Moments

Present moments are all you have. The past does not exist, nor does the future. I know I must be sounding a bit ethereal, but this is an important concept. For example, I know folks who have made a big mistake some-where in their business or personal lives and cannot let go of the negative feeling—the guilt—that remains with them. They carry the burden, and it takes a toll by reducing their energy, their once great attitude, and their overall initiative. They often change their personality and emotionally go into a fetal position around others.

We all make mistakes. In fact, it's been my experience that the people who achieve the most are likely making the most mistakes. The solution is to admit mistakes, learn from them, apply those lessons going forward—and then move on. Let it go. Let it be.

You have the ability to be fully engaged in your present moments, but when you are carrying guilt from your past or worry for your future—both negative emotions—you are no longer fully invested in your present moments. Therefore, you will not be nearly as effective as you could be.

Example

Some of my clients, when I am on their campus, will ask me to stay an extra day for mentoring their staff, and will give me an office for the day. Outside the office door, there is a calendar posted and folks can sign up to be mentored in blocks of 30 minutes.

This one gentleman—Vijay—was having a serious problem with his project and brought his project plan. He signed on for two consecutive blocks of 30 minutes each to ensure that we did not run out of time before he was sufficiently helped.

About 20 minutes into the session there was a knock on the door (Knock! Knock! Knock!). I shouted, *Yeah?* The door opens, and a lady tells Vijay that he is wanted on a conference call right now. She goes on to say, *... and by the way, both our VP and the client's VP are on the call—as well as several other senior managers.* The person left and closed the door.

Vijay immediately rose from his chair and moved toward the door. I asked him where he was going. He said, *You heard. I'm wanted on a conference call.* I suggested to Vijay to come back, sit down, and relax a moment—and he did. I said, *The people on the conference call probably don't even know that you have been found.*

I asked Vijay if he knew what the conference call was about. He said yes, that he had messed up and told me what the issue was. I said that he was right, he did mess up. But who doesn't from time to time?

I suggested he enter the call and take the following four actions:

1. *Admit you made a mistake.* This will immediately diffuse the situation. It's no fun for folks to kick you when you're down.
2. *State what you are going to do to fix the problem before someone directs you to do so or tells you how to do so.* This is called being *accountable.*
3. *State what you are going to do so that this problem does not happen again.* This is called being *professional.*
4. *Let it go!* Learn from the experience but do not be defined by it. Emotionally, let it go.

Vijay asked a few questions of me and was shortly on his way to the conference call.

I found out that afternoon that Vijay had taken my advice and implemented all four suggestions. I was quite proud of him.

What Would You Have Done?

Would you have taken my advice and pursued these actions? I have given this example to thousands of students over the years. A small minority say they would have followed through on all four items. About a third suggest they would have done the first three, but likely could not do the last item of letting it go. To be your best, you must learn from the experience and move on; otherwise, you are not fully invested in the moment; you are living in your past and worrying about your future.

Another Example

One day, while a project manager of a sizable, high-profile project, my boss walked into my office and informed me that a senior executive from headquarters was in town and planned to visit me in an hour to find out the status of my project. I would like to think that I'm a decent project manager, but with only one hour to prepare, it was insufficient time to update some presentation charts and chase down the project's latest status.

My hands started to sweat. But I immediately caught myself and decided that I did not have a choice over whether I will be presenting to this executive in one hour, but I do have a choice how I spend the next 59 minutes and 30 seconds in getting prepared. I chose to fully live in my present moments—fully concentrate—and prepare the *best I could!* I cannot do better than that!

Concentrate Fully in the Now

When you go to work each day, you can concentrate this much. (I am holding one hand above the other about one foot apart, about 30 centimeters.) But when you come to work living in the past—carrying guilt whether from your professional or personal life—or living in the future—worrying—it causes you to reduce your depth of concentration. (My bottom hand has moved up and now my hands are about 6 inches apart, about 15 centimeters.)

As I said, present moments are all we have. The past does not exist, nor does the future. If you try and live in either, then it will cause you to reduce your concentration and effectiveness in your present moments. To embrace this Power Skill, learn from the past, plan for the future, but live fully in the now if you want to perform your best.

Question

I have done things in my past that I regret and cannot let go of. I don't ever see me being able to control the harmful emotions I carry about those past events. Comments?

Answer

It is possible to learn to control your thoughts on such things. Do you really want to carry these burdens throughout your life? Of course not. If there is some restitution you can perform to make it right, then you can choose to go that route. Of course, you want to do the right thing. But know that you cannot change the past. Elements of it can still haunt you if you choose to dwell on them. Learn from those experiences and be the best version of yourself, but I caution you to not allow yourself to be negatively controlled by these events. If necessary, don't overlook obtaining professional counsel to help you overcome this. The 1970 Beatles hit song title gives a great clue on a technique that may help your healing by adopting the mantra *Let it be*.

9.   Don't Make It Personal or Take It Personally

It's all about what's best for the business. It's not personal. Don't take it so or make it so. Most of us have a challenging time applying this skill. We don't like losing. We don't like looking bad. We want things to go our way. We don't like speed bumps of interference. We don't want to be slowed down or redirected. Guess what? Get over it. These things happen to all of us and will continue to do so. The Power Skill here is the positive manner with which you deal with these occasions.

Examples

It's common for many of us to take things personal at work. Here are some examples:

- A co-worker disagrees with you on an issue
- People arrive late to your meeting
- You lost your issue in an escalation meeting
- You view that your promotion is overdue
- A deliverable to you is lower quality than expected
- A project member has been reassigned off your project
- A co-worker is late in replying to your request
- You feel pressed into working overtime
- You weren't invited to lunch with several co-workers
- Your project is cancelled after several months of difficult and dedicated work
- Two team members are unable to resolve an issue among themselves.

This list could be endless. There are so many experiences at work that a person could choose to take personally.

But here's the deal: Don't! As I said, it's not personal. Don't make it personal or take it personally. It's just business. Say it over and over a few times so the mantra sticks when you most need it to help you see situations from a business perspective. Maturely examine each event when it happens and respond in the most appropriate manner.

A Closer Look

Let's take a closer look at a few of these examples and apply good business sense when considering a response.

A Co-worker Disagrees With You on an Issue.   You should consider the co-worker's view. He or she could be right. Or there may be middle ground that's superior to your initial approach. Even if a consensus cannot be reached, maintaining open communications where other people's views are encouraged, welcomed, and considered can add significant value to the team's overall effectiveness.

People Arrive Late to Your Meeting.   Clearly, this can be quite annoying. However, a late arriver often has a legitimate reason for not arriving on time. Even you have been late to a meeting before. If a person is routinely tardy, then work with that person, and other appropriate staff as needed, to remedy the situation. Don't overlook potential aids such as starting your meetings 10 minutes after the hour so people can get to your meeting from their last meeting. And ending your meeting at least 10 minutes before the hour so they can be on time to their next meeting.

You Lost Your Issue in an Escalation.   I have found that with most escalations, both parties are right when looking at the issue from their points of view. Escalating an issue to higher levels of leadership is intended to resolve the issue based on what's best for the business—and the view higher up is often more objective. Now, if you lost the escalation because you were not fully prepared or convincing, then that is on you to learn from so the next escalation can benefit.

You View That Your Promotion Is Overdue.   Work with your boss to understand what you must do, if anything, to earn a promotion or salary increase. But even then, understand that the business may not be able to support any action at this time. Don't leave the impression of being a negative, difficult, or unreasonable employee. Maintain a positive attitude in all that you do to help sell your manager on the recognition you seek. In other words, take the high road.

Two Team Members Are Unable to Resolve an Issue Among Themselves.   I was mentoring a PM. On the way to a meeting, the PM and I came upon two team members in the hallway having a loud, heated, and nasty discussion. The PM decided that we should join them; a few minutes later, we headed off to our meeting. Once we were out of earshot, I asked her why she didn't take a position on the issue to help move it to closure. She said that had she taken a position, she would have alienated one of the team members. I told her that she alienated both by not taking a position. They would probably have preferred that she make a decision so they could move on. And it would not be her problem if one of them disagreed with her decision and took it personally. Doing so would indicate the team member's own professional immaturity.

Never avoid making a decision or taking a position on an issue because you fear alienating someone. As a leader, you must not be a fence sitter. You must demonstrate the backbone to help close decisions, when appropriate.

We just went through five of the items from our list, but you see where I am going with this. Approach each instance separately and maturely and with a clear head to determine the best business approach.

It Comes Down to What's Best for the Business

Some people tend to make things personal, and some tend to take things personally. As I said, doing so is a sign of professional immaturity. Professional immaturity harms successful business outcomes. Resist allowing others to draw you into a personal conflict versus a business conflict. Take the high road. Do things because they are the right business things to do, not because you or someone else takes things personally.

Whether intentionally or not, we have all been guilty of demonstrating professional immaturity on some occasion in our past. If you succumb to taking or making it personal, this can lead to harmed relationships with those you work as well as damaging to your career. When you can positively control your emotions, you will find that co-workers are more likely to want to work with you.

The most successful employees don't make things personal. Instead, they know it's just business and behave accordingly. You should care about success. You should work with passion and take ownership of everything that can affect your domain of responsibility. But in the end, when the dust has settled, it's all about what's best for the business.

Question

Should leaders hold back on expressing negative emotions such as anger?

Answer

The best leaders control their emotions. They keep the drama to a minimum and their effectiveness to a maximum. Unfiltered anger comes from a lack of self-control. Once the negative emotion has been unleashed, it is nearly impossible to put it back in the proverbial bottle without regrettable aftereffects. Having said this, I will add that there are times when expressing some anger in a controlled fashion can effectively send the message that you want delivered. Use this technique sparingly and with caution.

Question

A co-worker and I could not reach agreement on an issue affecting our work, as hard as we tried. I escalated the issue and won. The co-worker took the escalation personally. She now avoids me whenever she can. If we find ourselves in the same meeting, she never looks at me or includes me in conversation. What should I do? Everyone can see what's happening.

Answer

What you don't want to do is negatively talk about that person behind her back. If she finds you have, you will only make the relationship turn further south. My style is to visit privately with the co-worker. Start the meeting being complimentary about something positive about the person. It is usually easy to find such an item about anyone. Then let the person know that you initiated the past escalation because you viewed that you both were at a standstill and work had to resume. Tell the person that it was not personal, only business. You can ask the person what she thinks should have happened if she owned the company and two of her staff had this conflict.

Let the person know that it is your hope that you both can put this behind you and carry on amicably. My experience is that this exercise will usually improve the relationship. On the off chance that it doesn't, and you are able to satisfactorily get your job done, let it go. Move on. It happens.

If the coworker's attitude is harming your ability to get your job done, you must address this further. Obtain counsel from your team leader or boss as to where to proceed from here.

10.   Embrace Integrity in All That You Do

Integrity. Listen to your inner voice and treat it as the wise and trusted friend it is. People who consistently and predictably practice integrity are typically the most respected and admired people in an organization.

Integrity Defined

I view that integrity is not an option. More than ever, the business world needs leaders who routinely embrace integrity. Simply put, *integrity* is knowing the difference between right and wrong and choosing the right action. You have a great internal compass for knowing right from wrong. As a leader, your integrity is indicative of your character. Use it to build your success and the success of those you lead or work among. Demonstrate integrity in every behavior you show, decision you make, and action you take.

Do not support or condone illegal or unethical behavior. If you find yourself unable to decide what the right thing to do is in a particular situation, sometimes it can help to discuss the issue with a trusted third party to ensure that you are not too close to the issue and can see it for what it really is. We all make mistakes, but when we make mistakes in areas of ethics and legality, the stakes are much higher both for us and our management upward.

Don't Ever Give in to Illegal or Unethical Behavior

A simple rule: Don't ever give in to illegal or unethical behavior. Never! Why do I bring this up? Because most of us will encounter illegal or unethical behavior at least a half-dozen times in our careers. It may not be common, but it's not uncommon.

First: Distinguishing Right From Wrong

What should you do if you encounter illegal or unethical behavior? First, distinguishing right from wrong may not always be easy; sometimes we encounter gray areas. Don't always assume purposeful wrongdoing. When you encounter a suspicious situation, you can quietly research it and ask questions. Also consider seeking help from a corporate ombudsman, legal counsel, or other trusted source.

Second: Never Support Improper Behavior

Never support someone who engages in illegal or unethical behavior. If you do, expect to go down with it. And if you think that the wrongdoer will protect you, think again. People who commit illegal or unethical activities are notorious for selling out those who are loyal to them.

You Have Several Choices

If you encounter illegal or unethical behavior, you have several choices; however, all those choices have a potential downside.

- Do nothing
- Mitigate the situation before it develops into something much more serious

- Distance yourself from the behavior by leaving the organization or company
- Be a whistle-blower.

Do Nothing

If you do nothing—in effect, stick your head in the sand—this can be considered supporting and condoning the behavior. Because of your knowledge of the activity, you may even be considered an accomplice to the misdeeds. Furthermore, you might find yourself consumed with anxiety, constantly looking over your shoulder for fear that something or someone is *gaining on you*. Not a good way to live a happy and quality life.

Mitigate the Situation

By mitigating the situation, I mean if another person or group is *considering* doing something that is illegal or unethical, you might be able to convince them to stop before any real harm has occurred. But if they choose to move forward, you may now be seen as a threat, and you could be in harm's way.

Distance Yourself

As far as distancing yourself by leaving the organization or company, leaving is not always so easy. There may not be another job for you elsewhere in the company, or if there is, you may have to move to another location which can be expensive and oh-so inconvenient. Quitting the company and finding another job, of course, can be a big hardship. Furthermore, the job that you are leaving could be a job that you have worked hard for, and you really enjoy. By the way, who is to say that the organization or new company you flee to will not have a similar problem there?

Be a Whistle-Blower

Then there is the option of whistle-blower. Many folks would consider this taking the high road. You are exposing illegal or unethical behavior and working within the system to improve your workplace. But what about those people around you that you are exposing? Justice can have a slow way of being served—if it is served at all—and you get to work around these folks in the meantime. They can make your job and life unbearable.

Be an Anonymous Whistle-Blower

What's that? How about being an anonymous whistle-blower? That's an option. But be prepared for the worst-case scenario, in which your anonymity is eventually lost as you become more involved in exposing the behavior.

Don't Allow Yourself to Get Drawn in

Nobody likes these options. Again, confiding in a trusted third party and talking through the options can be helpful. But as I said earlier, whatever you do, do not allow yourself to be drawn into illegal or unethical behavior, or you will surely go down with it. We are talking here about your character, your career, and your future.

Example

Armando is a project manager. He has had many moments where he is uncertain as to what the correct course of action should be from an integrity perspective. He doesn't feel good about obtaining legal counsel because he's afraid someone will make too big a deal about it. Armando also does not want to get anyone in trouble or burn any bridges. Consequently, he quietly allows some things to happen under his watch, *But, hey!*—Armando rationalizes, *these things are normal and happen all the time.* Here are a few events that Armando easily recalls:

- A customer, vendor, and contractor—all of whom can benefit from his position—secretly give him gifts
- He occasionally hears, *It will turn out fine as long as no one knows about it*

- He notices that many supplies are disappearing without any accountability
- He is asked to charge for some services and products that he did not need or receive, and he will get a cash kickback of 25 percent.

Armando is a little nervous recalling these events because they are getting more frequent, and he's beginning to be concerned that someone might slip up and some or all these misdeeds will become exposed.

Listen to Your Instincts

Here's a dead giveaway: When your conscience or instincts say you would not want this to appear on the front page of your local newspaper, or perhaps, you would not want your mom or family to know, it's time for an integrity check. Listen to your great instincts.

Your leaders rightfully expect integrity to be part and parcel of your commitments to them and to the business. Don't risk your reputation, your career, damaging relationships, or worse condoning or participating in illegal or unethical behavior. The integrity you demonstrate is indicative of your character. As the old saying goes, *Listen to the whispers of your conscience as if they were shouts.*

Question

I think you make too much of integrity. If I infrequently look the other way when something illegal or unethical is going down, I can't get too bothered. This is just part of the world we live in. Comments?

Answer

It can be a slippery slope. One look-away can easily morph into several. This is why I say integrity should not be an option. By the way, if you owned the company, would you accept this behavior? If you say yes, my experience is that both your company's potential and your character will eventually suffer, perhaps beyond repair.

CHAPTER 3

Be a Role Model by Your Leadership

This category reveals the next 6 of the 24 foundational Power Skills:

11. Think like a leader
12. Treat others as you would like to be treated
13. Trust but verify; inspect what you expect
14. Understand and practice empowerment
15. Treat all project members equally
16. Promote diversity, equity, and inclusivity.

11.   Think Like a Leader

Do you know your company's most cherished asset? My experience is that most people do not. That's sad to me because it can be problematic of why many organizations have stalled in their growth and effectiveness.

Company's Most Cherished Asset

Here are some common answers to what a company's most valued asset is. All are important, but only the last is correct.

People? Many companies mistakenly say so in their core beliefs.

Profit? Obviously important to a for-profit company, and sound financials are a sign of effective management even for nonprofits, academic institutions, and public sector entities.

Products and services? Your products and services are magnets for clients.

Clients? Without them, the company has no future.

Intellectual property? Past investments help secure future success.

Brand? How will customers know you otherwise?

Marketing? The only way to tell customers about your products and services.

Cash flow? Solid companies can pay their bills and invest in their future.

Productivity? An ever-rising bar.

Quality? Of course, this is important.

Creativity and ingenuity? A company cannot rest on its laurels.

Integrity? Getting warmer …

Leaders? BINGO! A company's most cherished asset is its leaders; it's leadership!

Leaders Foretell a Company's Success

A company's leaders foretell that company's success. If a company has mediocre leaders and the best employees, it will be a mediocre force in its industry. However, a company with the best leaders and mediocre employees will be a formidable force in its industry. Yes, formidable. It's all about leadership. Interestingly, companies with the best leaders don't have mediocre employees. Employees rise to the expectations of their leaders.

Think Like a Leader

Leaders place the responsibility and accountability squarely on their own shoulders. My focus of leadership is quite simple, yet far-reaching: *It's not about the ability of those around you to lead; it's about your ability to lead regardless of what is happening around you.*

If you worked in my organization and came to me and said that you cannot be successful because of the weak support—weak leadership—around you, I would ask you what *you* are doing despite that which is happening around you. You are not a victim unless you choose to be.

Example

David works for me and is a project manager. His project has just ended, and it failed. I don't mean that it didn't complete. It did. It's just that it completed late, over budget, and with low quality. David and I meet to discuss what happened on the project and what lessons we can learn.

In the mist of the discussion, David stands by two sentences that are not true; yet I hear these sentences dozens of times a year from project managers and other leaders in his situation:

1. *It wasn't my fault.*
2. *There was nothing I could do about it.*

It's Not My Fault

If you work for me, it's always your fault—you are always accountable. I prefer things to be my fault; that way, I typically have a lot of latitude to avoid or correct the situation. Your worst hardship is if it truly was not your fault because you can lose flexibility and control.

Nothing I Could Do

As for David saying that there was nothing he could do to fix the problem, there are always things that a person can do. They may not like their options, but options, nonetheless, do exist.

But going back to David, before I could say anything, he asserted that the problem was the vendor, and that the vendor was half-way around the world in Asia. (David resides in North America.) He went on to say that the vendor had three deliverables, which the vendor said would be on schedule, but each was late. Furthermore, each deliverable was low quality even though they were committed to be high quality. So, David again says: *As you can see it wasn't my fault and there was nothing I could do about it.*

If It Is to Be, It Is Up to Me

I then said to David that I do not recall during the project you coming to me and requesting funding to fly to the vendor's location and turn the problem around. David quickly replied that the vendor does not want him over there messing around in the vendor's business. I said, *I don't care what the vendor wanted. The vendor signed a contract and you, David, are my agent for success.* Then I stated 10 two-letter words:

If it is to be, it is up to me.

Meaning that if it is to be then it is up to David to make it happen.

Effective Leaders Are Looking for Solutions

Most leaders I know—and I know many hundreds and have worked around thousands—would not have thought to consider flying halfway around the world at great expense of time and budget to turn this problem around. I am not saying that this is the best option—it depends on options already considered—and what's best for the business. But this is how a truly effective leader thinks: Not about how little control they have or the obstacles that may seem overwhelming, but what can be done to mitigate them. My experience is that, in examples like this, the squeaky wheel typically gets the proverbial oil and visiting the vendor almost always can improve the situation.

Remember: It's not about the ability of those around you to lead; it's about your ability to lead regardless of what is happening around you. As a leader, you are your company's most cherished asset.

Question

Do you believe that leaders have a duty to serve those that they lead?

Answer

Yes. The best leaders see their role as predominantly serving, developing, and nurturing others rather than focusing on themselves. If those who are led are ever to reach their potential within an organization, then it's their leaders that will create the environment that supports that success. This thinking falls within the purview of the concept of *servant leadership*.

12. Treat Others as You Would Like to Be Treated

This Power Skill may be the most obvious, but it still needs to be high-lighted. People are not objects, commodities, or machines. We seek and require to be treated with respect, dignity, and nurturing. Nor are we low maintenance. We have great aspirations and, therefore, high needs. In fact, we are high maintenance whether we like it or not or admit it or not.

Remarkably Similar

When you get past the surface of what we each look like—we are all remarkably similar. We all want the same things from life: we want to be loved and appreciated; we want safety, security, and health; we want to contribute, to achieve; we want to dream and pursue those dreams to their imagined end.

Golden Rule

The core principle underlying effective interpersonal communications is the Golden Rule: *Treat others as you would like to be treated.* There is no better rule to follow when working with or serving others.

I commonly hear people say that they work alongside difficult people, people who can be rude, indifferent, demeaning, short-tempered, impatient, thoughtless, disrespectful, to name a few. Yes, I am probably defining your behavior once upon a time. We have all lapsed into this mode. However, most of us have learned to better control our responses when the need arises. After a while, we may not need to work so hard at being more respectful of others—eventually it becomes second nature to act more maturely and respectful when the need avails itself.

When you are faced with negative behavior, I suggest that you *not* retaliate with similar behavior. If you do, then the poor behaviors will continue forever and likely what's left of the relationship will deteriorate. Instead, I suggest you take the high road and respond in a manner that you would wish the person had originally adopted. My experience is that, in short order, the offending person will pick up on your grace and maturity and begin to express themselves in a similar way.

Will this always work out for the best? No. But it will more times than not. To become the person you most choose to be, you need to control you and the narrative that you want to project. In the infrequent cases where the Golden Rule is not embraced, the situation may need to be confronted to turn it around.

People and organizations who routinely follow the Golden Rule will reach a comfortable and productive harmony that will inspire people to look forward to working together.

Example

Let's look at an example of treating others with the respect that we wish for ourselves.

Nicole is a member of a project. She maintains a challenging work schedule and does her best to keep her overtime hours to a minimum. She prides herself in being consistent and predictable in working with others. Here are some examples of the practices she strives to implement:

- Return most phone calls and texts by the end of the day
- Return most e-mails/messages by the end of the day
- Arrive to meetings on time, whether mine or another's
- When appropriate, give others my undivided attention
- Speak up if I disagree or show support if I agree
- Meet my commitments
- If I suspect that a commitment will be missed, immediately inform the affected party, and work out a mitigation plan
- Do not escalate an issue without first attempting to work it out with the respective party
- Share important news directly with the affected party before they find out the news from a third source
- Do not speak ill of others unless privately with that person
- Do not condone or support illegal or unethical behavior
- Do not lie or distort the truth
- Maintain a business philosophy; do not take things personally or make them personal.

Are some of these ideas starting to look familiar?

Lesson

What is the primary lesson here? Treat others as you would like them to treat you. Nicole's list of example practices makes it clear that she endorses the Golden Rule philosophy. It's a simple rule that can develop and nurture great relationships. The best-run projects and organizations—and often those with the highest morale—typically are those where individuals demonstrate a basic respect for one another.

Quote by Maya Angelou

I find it helpful to keep in mind the quote by Maya Angelou, an American poet and civil rights activist. Great words to live by!

I've learned that people will forget what you said, people will forget what you did, but people will never forget how you made them feel.

Question

You say that the core principle underlying respect for others is the Golden Rule. Are you making a religious statement?

Answer

No. I respect and honor each person's right to believe as they choose if it does not interfere with the well-being of others. I happen to find the Golden Rule to be, by far, the best philosophy to embrace in working and living with others. Projects and organizations benefit greatly by its application.

13. Trust but Verify; Inspect What You Expect

As a leader, don't trust that things are progressing smoothly across your team or will work out okay on their own. Strive to build trust among project stakeholders, but insist on metrics, checks and balances, and other tools to ensure outcomes are being met. Many leaders think that inspecting what you expect is micromanaging. It's not. It's good leadership.

Micromanaging is telling someone what to do, when to do it, how to do it, and so forth. Micromanaging should only be used in rare instances such as in an emergency or in a limited capacity with an underperforming team member.

Blind Trust Can Be a Big Mistake Unless It Has Been Earned

The phrase *inspect what you expect* has been around for a long time, but its message goes unheeded by many project managers. Who hasn't had a project where a team member insists that things are fine? That the delivery will be on schedule and will meet the quality expected? But then the delivery date arrives, and it's not ready. Blind trust can be a huge mistake.

Example

I was asked to perform a review on a troubled project. The project originally was planned to run about eight months but continued for nearly twice that without convincing data on when it will be complete. After a project review and my recommendations, the project was replanned and estimated to be complete in another six months.

One month later, I asked the project manager, Anika, what were her top three priorities? After some thought, she eventually identified her top three. Her top priority was to validate the long list of product requirements with the client to ensure that both parties had the same interpretation.

This was a new six-week activity that she had assigned to Juan; he was just starting the fifth week. I asked if Juan was on schedule. Anika said, *Yes.* I asked how she knew that. Anika said that Juan, a senior-level project member, repeatedly announced in the weekly project tracking meetings that he is on schedule. Because there were only two weeks left of the six-week activity, I asked Anika if Juan and the client would work over the one remaining weekend available if it is necessary to protect their commitments to the schedule. Anika said that she had full trust and confidence in Juan. After all, she said, *Juan is a professional.*

As it turned out, Juan was *four weeks late* in completing the planned six-week activity and did not work any weekends. Furthermore, Juan said the activity *should be completed by next week* for the next four weeks. Ouch!

Avoid Being Micromanaged

If your clients or senior management micromanage your projects, it's for a reason: You invited it by your inaction. When a project member has made a commitment to you either directly or by way of the project plan, what are you doing to ensure that the words *I am on schedule* are true and meet your expectations? If you don't inspect the work of others as needed, your work will rightly become the focus of inspection.

As the project manager, you are the commander of your ship. If a failure occurs, you are responsible and accountable—even if someone else misses a commitment—the failure occurred under your command. As Albert Einstein was quoted, *Insanity is doing the same thing over and over but expecting different results.*

Progress Must Be Measurable Against a Plan

Project members must know what they are being held accountable for, that is, what you expect from them. These expectations must be measurable. Project members then routinely must report progress against those measured expectations.

Don't Trust Anyone

As a general principle, don't trust anyone. Question everything. Assume nothing. It's not personal. It's business. It's good business. How many times must a project manager get drawn into this trap? Requiring a trackable plan and routine progress reports demonstrates strong leadership.

We Tend to Be Eternal Optimists

In most cases, it is not okay to trust that others will do as they say. Most people working on projects will not intentionally lie, but most of us are eternal optimists. We mean well, but when faced with a problem we can paint ourselves into a corner and inadvertently cause problems for others. As I said earlier, if you have a dependency on someone for something, it is up to *you* to ensure that you have an appropriate plan for tracking the progress of the dependency.

Listen to Your Instincts

Here again, we are rightly discussing your instincts. When your instincts alert you that there is something suspect about a commitment, trust those instincts. We all have remarkably good instincts. Too many of us are too soft to act upon those instincts. Be fair, but firm. Inspect what you expect. Your projects will benefit greatly, not to mention your career.

Question

As a leader, is it ever okay to trust a team member when it comes to his or her commitments?

Answer

It is, but only after the team member has earned that trust through his or her repeated actions. Even then you could be fooled. However, when a leader and a team member have developed that trust, their relationship becomes stronger and the morale higher.

14.   Understand and Practice Empowerment

Empowerment is an overused word these days, but it's an underused concept. Empowerment, to me, is three things:

1. Understanding your job
2. Taking ownership of your job
3. Doing whatever is necessary—within legal and ethical parameters—to accomplish that job.

Understanding Your Job

It is my experience that most people don't really understand their job. If they did, they would be more effective in accomplishing that job. If you are not sure of your job, I suggest you *NOT* ask your boss. Instead, take one sheet of paper and write on it in high-level bullets what you view your job to be. Then take that sheet and use it as a basis for discussion with your boss. Although your boss should have already clarified your job to you, the initiative you take in creating these talking points and engaging in discussion will not only help you to understand what constitutes superior performance, your boss will respect your initiative in driving the discussion.

Taking Ownership of Your Job

The second part of the three-part definition of empowerment is: *Taking ownership of your job.* This can be demonstrated by coming to work each day with the mindset that you own the company, and your company is defined by your domain of responsibility. If you take on your job each day as a business owner with the mindset that if you are not successful then you will be out of a job with no cash flow, then success takes on a very real and vivid necessity.

Doing Whatever Is Necessary

The third part of the three-part definition of empowerment is: *Doing whatever is necessary to accomplish your job*—providing it is legal and ethical. This thinking can add a new dimension to your performance. It will help you look for resourceful ways to solve problems rather than searching for excuses why they are too difficult to solve.

Example

I have a client in Germany, where I have conducted several training classes and I talk about such things as empowerment and what it really means. In one class, as I was discussing the empowerment topic, a student said that one of my past students—her name is Heidi—took to heart what I had taught. I asked for an example. He said that Heidi needed to discuss an issue with our Group Manager and then obtain his signature. This Group Manager has 17,000 people working under his direction. But Heidi was unable to get on his calendar because he was so busy. He worked a lot of overtime but was almost always inaccessible with closed-door meetings and travelling.

The student went on to say that Heidi had an idea based on my teachings of *do whatever is necessary to accomplish your job—providing it is legal and ethical.* Heidi discovered where the Group Manager parked his car when he came to work, and what his car looked like. She brought a fold-up chair to work and at the standard quitting time, she settled in alongside his car and waited for him. The Group Manager appeared at his car at 10 o'clock that evening. Heidi was able to have the discussion and obtain his approval signature.

Applause

I asked if anyone knew where Heidi was at this moment. Someone did. I asked how quickly you think you can have her in this classroom. He said possibly within five minutes. I told the class to take a 10-minute break. When the class started back up, there was Heidi. I asked everyone to give her a round of applause—that she practices precisely what I am talking about: Doing whatever is necessary to accomplish your job, providing it is legal and ethical.

Use Good Judgment

As a sidebar, I should add that a person must use good judgment. In Heidi's case, she worked on a safe campus and sitting in the parking lot after hours was not considered a safety risk. She also sensed that the Group Manager respected employees who are resourceful in getting their job done. She was right. Most senior management would respect such resourcefulness. Heidi understood and practiced empowerment.

By the way, I knew the Group Manager. He personally had invited me to teach many of the Power Skills in this book. He also respected the initiative of Heidi.

Question

This example doesn't feel right to me. It seems wrong to surprise an executive late at night who is likely exhausted and just wants to get home. Comments?

Answer

Most employees will likely be able to get on their executive's calendar. But this example demonstrates that there may be times when things don't work in your favor by following standard protocols. If you are assigned to do a job and your success relies on a discussion and signature from an executive whose presence is impossible for you to schedule in the customary way, what do you do? Throw your arms up, whine, and get zinged on your performance because you could not meet your commitments? Of course not. You do what you need to do—providing it is legal and ethical—to meet your commitments so your company can prosper. This is what this book is all about: Power Skills to embrace to be an exceptional performer. You must decide your level of adoption of these Power Skills. The more Power Skills revealed in this book that you choose to adopt, the greater effect you will have on your performance, career, and the success of your organization.

Question

When you say *Do whatever is necessary to accomplish your job—providing it is legal and ethical,* I feel like it's too easy to exceed my authority ... and that's not a good thing. I don't have the power assigned to me to be pushing the envelope in making things happen. I consciously work at staying in my lane. Am I being too cautious?

Answer

You get to be whoever you choose. Having said that, I believe the current way you choose to think will significantly hold you back in your career and life. For example, when was the last time your management called you on the proverbial carpet for exceeding your authority? Was it within the last week? Last month? Last year? Ever?

My experience is that most people cannot recall a time when they were singled out for exceeding their authority. This speaks volumes about their current performance and realizing their potential performance. My experience is that you have far more power than you realize. The issue is you are not exploiting that power.

15. Treat All Project Members Equally

As simple and straightforward as this advice may sound—*treat all project members equally*—my experience is that most project managers and leaders do not practice it—but should.

Diverse Groups on a Project

Many projects today are made up of at least four diverse groups: company personnel, client personnel, vendors, and contractors. Once people are assigned to a project, regardless of where they hail from, they must all be treated the same. No exceptions!

The focus should be on the overall project, the commitments from each team, and the corresponding actions that each project member performs toward achieving assigned activities. The project manager sees everyone as a project member and will work with each person and group as if they were personnel from the same project team—*because they are!*

Everyone Is Held Accountable

All project members, regardless of where they come from or whom they report to, must be held accountable for their commitments. Each team is expected to have plans, commit to those plans, and track according to those plans. If any team is in trouble, or headed that way, the project manager, if needed, initiates the attention required to help the team get back on plan. Each team is held just as accountable for its commitments as any other team.

A Project Suffers When Preferential Treatment Is Given to Any Group or Person

I commonly see project managers treat the client's personnel assigned to the project with kid gloves—quick to cut them slack at every turn. I often see vendors treated as if they are a *sealed box* that cannot be tampered with, their whims easily accepted as *cast in stone* with little or no chance of altering. I see contractors treated like second-class members of the team, where project information is often withheld from them—information that they need to function fully as members of the project. And I often see company employees treated harshly based on the view that they are the most accessible project members and, arguably, the easiest to lean on.

Example

Project ABC consists of members from all four groups: company personnel, client personnel, vendors, and contractors. The project completes substantially late. This causes a great hardship to the client, who brings litigation against the company that managed the project—the same company that provided the project manager.

The project manager respectfully confronts the client executive who initiated the legal action and asks why he is suing. After all, says the project manager, the project's primary problems were poor performance from your team—the client team. The client executive asked why he was not informed that his team was causing problems on the project. He also asked why the project manager allowed the problems to continue.

The project manager said he knows who butters his bread, so he had consistently cut the client team slack when their commitments were late or low quality. The project manager also says that it's not good business to bite the hand that feeds you.

The client executive responded that the client team does not butter your bread, I do as the client executive who signed the contract. He went on to say that the client team was a team of the project and its people just happened to work for the client company. The client executive also said that had he known that the primary problems on the project were from his own organization—meaning the client team—he would have worked swiftly to correct the problems. But no one routinely informed him. Therefore, the executive sued for breach of contract due to the missed commitments.

Only as Strong as Its Weakest Link

This scenario shows an example where the project manager treated the client personnel assigned to the project in ways special over other project members. This scenario is all too common. It is vital to remember that a project's success depends on the success of each project member. As the saying goes, *A chain is only as strong as its weakest link.* Any one member or team can harm the project. An effective project manager recognizes this and works consistently, firmly, and unbiasedly across all members of a project to ensure that the project completes successfully, addressing weak links whenever and wherever they are identified.

Question

As a project manager, I don't feel I have the authority to treat all project members and teams the same—only those that work for my company such as company employees and company contractors. I don't have authority over client and vendor teams. Comments?

Answer

Listen to you. You are, in effect, saying that client personnel and vendor personnel can run roughshod over the project's outcome because they are protected from your scrutiny. You must lay down these rules at the start of the project. If you haven't, then negotiate them now. Do not be intimidated by any teams or team members on the project. The project cannot be successful unless all teams and project members are successful. Go do your job! Everyone is counting on you!

16.   Promote Diversity, Equity, and Inclusion

As a leader of a team, project, department, or organization or as someone who works with others, you are in a position to promote diversity, equity, and inclusion (DEI). Let's briefly define these terms. These definitions were mostly taken from Ideal, a talent intelligence system, on their website: Ideal.com/diversity-equity-inclusion/. I found these definitions to be among the most simple and straightforward.

Diversity Definition

Diversity is about recognizing and accepting the inherent differences among people. For example, common types of diversity center around race, age, nationality, ethnicity, gender identity, education, spiritual and religious beliefs, marital status, socioeconomic status, and union affiliation, to name a few. But diversity is less about what makes people different and more about understanding, accepting, and valuing those differences.

Equity Definition

Equity is about creating opportunity and advancement for all those different people. It's also about fairness and treating everyone justly—which is sometimes missing from the equation.

Inclusion Definition

Inclusion is the extent to which team members, employees, and other people feel a sense of belonging and value within a given organizational setting. Inclusion is a workplace culture that reaches out to all people.

Benefits of Promoting All Three

There are many benefits from embracing DEI. For example, when employees feel included, they are more engaged and feel more appreciated and respected. Their commitment and trust increase. They tend to work smarter and produce higher quality work. Employee morale increases, a wider hiring talent pool emerges, and business results such as profitability increase. (This material was largely drawn from the article "10 Benefits of Diversity, Equity, and Inclusion in the Workplace," August 11, 2021, by Elijah, www.themissionhr.com.) Embracing DEI can also be a magnet for more diverse clients.

Examples

Let's look at some examples of a leader promoting DEI:

- Giving each team member an opportunity to fulfill team member roles and responsibilities
- Holding team members equally accountable for their assignments

- Making a point to listen to all team members, not just the vocal ones
- Recognizing and rewarding all team members fairly
- Demonstrating no special treatment for any team members
- Promoting diverse groups for problem identification and resolution brainstorming
- Soliciting ideas from the entire team for creating a team's core/shared values so everyone has a role in defining the team's culture
- Being a change agent for fairly promoting diversity, equity, and inclusiveness at every opportunity
- Implementing an open-door policy where DEI concepts and practices can be discussed
- Periodically conducting surveys to gain perspective on potential biases that need to be addressed
- Seeking training on unconscious bias for yourself and team members
- Acknowledging holidays of all cultures
- Recognizing that every team member can bring a different perspective
- Seeking to discover the specialness of each team member, especially those that are less like you
- Listening without judging while asking follow-up questions to better understand an issue
- Being humble in acknowledging that you have more to learn and are open to other views
- Becoming a role model for promoting and valuing DEI.

Be the Change You Seek From Others

The workplace and world are changing. Fast. I would argue that the changes are almost always for the good as they are considered, tested, and adopted. Most people tend to do things because the business demands it. But with DEI, it also greatly benefits humanity. As a leader, you are in the best position to promote these three concepts. This is a great opportunity to be on the leading edge of change. It's not necessarily easy, but it is essential if you want to build and nurture the best teams to take on the ever-challenging future. However, as I mentioned earlier, it is important to implement DEI justly and fairly to all.

Question

Is it wrong for a person to hang out at work with only people of their own ethnicity?

Answer

A person should be free to choose the people they wish to hang with at work if it does not interfere with their performance and commitments to a project or organization. An exception relates to someone in a leadership position such as a project manager or manager. For example, if a manager only hangs out (e.g., lunch, idle chat time) with people of their own ethnicity, yet they have people of other ethnicities reporting to them, then there can be the *perception* of impropriety; that is, their other employees may believe, rightly or wrongly, that there is potential bias going on and that they are at a disadvantage for opportunities, promotions, awards, salary increases, and so on, compared to the *chosen* group. Leaders must play by different rules because of their positions of power and influence in the organization and company.

CHAPTER 4

Use Constructive Interactions to Improve

This category reveals the next 4 of the 24 foundational Power Skills:

17. Seek out a mentor
18. Evaluate yourself daily
19. Promote mutual relationships
20. Treat your customer as if it matters.

17. Seek Out a Mentor

A *mentor* is a trusted counselor whose primary objective is to help a mentee be more effective in a specific area of interest—to help develop the mentee's potential.

Draw Strength From Those Who Have Gone Before Us

There is no better way to learn the application of a profession—a craft—than with a mentor by your side when needed. There is no better way! Not classes. Not workshops. Not articles or books. Even on-the-job training is not as effective. Many of us have learned and practiced bad habits for years, not realizing that there are better practices out there. A mentor can help you discover your possibilities. We learn much more and far faster when we can draw strength from those who have gone before us.

Example

Here's a situation I have played out with thousands of students over the years. What would be your position?

If a major aerospace company was looking to build the next-generation commercial aircraft of a multigenerational fleet, would I be a great candidate—based on what you know about me—to run that project? I briefly inform the students of my rich background in project and program management and leadership: published eight books and over 150 articles in respected publishing venues, instructed hundreds of workshops, developed over 20 online courses in use today, and reviewed over 100 projects in trouble—just for starters. Typically, a class is split 50 to 50.

For those who said I would be a great candidate, I appreciate your confidence in me. However, I would *not* be a great candidate. The reason is my lack of domain knowledge on aerospace projects. Although I have strong domain knowledge in several industries, aerospace is not one of them. I don't know what I don't know. I would not know all the right questions to ask throughout the project. Nor can I rely on the project members to make up for my weak domain knowledge.

If the best project manager—typically called program manager in this case—could achieve concept to first flight in three years, it would likely take me 3.5 to 4 years. However, I would like to think I am a reasonably quick study. On the next-generation project, I believe I could achieve flight in three years or very possibly less.

A Highly Qualified Mentor Can Be the Game Changer

But here's the kicker: Based on my leadership and project skills, I believe I could achieve first flight in three years on my first project, providing I could handpick a mentor who was both an outstanding aerospace technical expert and process expert in building next-generation commercial aircraft. This person would be my right hand and would make up for what I don't know. We would be a formidable team. See the power of the right mentor at the right time?

Best Mentors

The best mentors are seasoned leaders who often have learned the hard way—by making mistakes and learning and growing from those painful experiences as well as from their successes. Mentors often give you different perspectives, fresh eyes, new ideas; they enable you to see the forest, not just the knots in the trees.

What Would You Do?

If you question the benefit of a mentor, picture this: If you have years of project management experience, think back to how much a project management mentor—the right mentor under the right circumstances—would have helped you accelerate your learning of both hard and soft project management skills, avoid some hefty mistakes, and as a side benefit, move your career ahead sooner.

If you have limited project management experience, how often have you wished you could have access to someone with the right answers the first time? A mentor's advice can greatly benefit your career and help protect your projects from *crash and burn*.

Most Mentees Know the Right Answer

I mentor about a dozen people at any point in time. They are project and program managers, team leaders, managers, senior managers, and anybody who wants to learn and grow at an accelerated pace. When I get a call from a mentee with a problem, the mentee knows that I will be asking them what they think is the best approach. To my initial surprise when I started mentoring many years ago, about 80 percent of folks knew the right answer to the question they were asking. But just getting reassurance—the validation—that they are on the correct path was all the inspiration they needed to continue.

By the way, the people I mentor have learned far faster than I did earlier in my career. I never truly had a mentor, but if I had to do it again, I would have pursued this valuable tool.

A Mentor Offers Great Benefit

The bottom line is that having a mentor can greatly benefit a person's skill development and effectiveness, increase their value to the organization, and enrich their satisfaction with their chosen craft. Whatever your craft and skills, there is always more to learn from others. In the long run, you're likely to be very pleased that you did reach out to accelerate and raise the bar on your personal growth. We are far more effective when we ask for help from, and stand on the shoulders of, those who have gone before us.

Question

I would like to find a mentor in my organization, but I don't want that person to share my weaknesses with my boss. Your thoughts?

Answer

Communications between the mentor and the mentee must be strictly confidential for the mentee to gain the most benefit from the mentor. It should be a penalty-free relationship with a relaxed, trusted, and open atmosphere. There are no dumb questions. Make sure your mentor understands this before you engage.

18.   Evaluate Yourself Daily

When your day ends, the dust settles and you can see the results of your efforts and actions, what picture emerges? Is it clear and concise? Does it support a vision? Or is it fuzzy, in disarray, and lacking purpose?

Here's a technique that can help you grow your leadership skills and become more effective today than you were yesterday—and even more effective tomorrow than you are today.

Imagine what your performance would be like in one year if you began each workday with evaluating your performance from the past workday and looked for ways to apply those lessons going forward. This daily evaluation may only take 5 to 15 minutes, yet the longer-term payback in improving your performance can be substantial.

Evaluate Yesterday

Here's how it works. At the start of each workday—when you are at your freshest—spend a few quiet moments reflecting on your performance from the day before. Do three things:

1. List the top three things that you could have done better that day
2. List the top three things you did that you were especially pleased with
3. Identify what you can do today (the next day) to apply those lessons.

For example, if, in hindsight, you believed that you were rude to someone in a meeting yesterday, you could apologize today. Another example might be if you weren't as prepared as you thought you should be for a presentation, you can list areas for improvement that you can review for the next presentation.

Applying Lessons Learned

Basing today's actions on yesterday's behavior enables you to adjust via lessons learned. Moreover, this immediate self-assessment can help you recover from missteps while the trail is still warm, and deliberate recovery actions can have the most beneficial impact.

Performing the adjustments routinely—preferably each day—can have a strikingly positive impact on your effectiveness as a leader. We often avoid self-assessments, especially if they are routine, because we prefer to avoid any reminders of our so-called *failures*. But, as professionals, these self-assessments are essential for our continued growth, maturity, and effectiveness.

Share the Exercise With a Friend

Even more powerful, occasionally include a trusted friend or mentor in assessing your past behaviors and discuss how best to apply the resulting lessons to present and future actions. If you and a friend perform this exercise with one another once a week, you will likely see a positive impact emerging over a relatively short period.

Lead Yourself as well as Others

This best-practice technique of evaluating yourself daily may seem simple, but it is disarmingly effective. It can continuously and dramatically improve your leadership effectiveness. Routinely applying this technique allows old habits to be questioned and immediately replaced by more effective *new* habits.

Quote

I am reminded of a saying by Thomas J. Watson, an industrialist, entrepreneur, and former chairman of IBM:

> *Nothing so conclusively proves a man's ability to lead others as what he does from day to day to lead himself.*

Question

Should I inform my boss that I evaluate myself daily?

Answer

I would. I only see an upside in your boss knowing about your desire for continuous personal improvement. I have found two things to be true.

1. People who evaluate themselves daily are almost always surprised how much they learn about themselves.
2. Typically, less than five percent of people evaluate themselves daily.

19.   Promote Mutual Relationships

Most people can get their job done by having only mediocre co-worker relationships. If there is reasonable mutual respect, good things can get done. However, when your relationships are viewed as strong, more can be done in less time and with less stress on the players. Your day not only becomes more productive, but it's also more pleasant and you probably like your job more. Often you need strong alliances to help accomplish your work mission in the most proficient manner.

Examples

Although good working relationships can happen serendipitously with just a little effort, being more deliberate in forming bonds and networking can strengthen those relationships significantly. Here are some examples that can help build stronger relationships. These ideas can apply to co-workers, clients, senior management, or most anyone else that you have a need to build a strong relationship with.

- *Make lunch dates once or twice a week.* Make a habit to invite at least one different person each week. Get to know your co-workers and give them the opportunity to know you. Personally invest in each other's success.
- *Briefly linger after some group meetings.* Take the time to thank someone for their support or let them know that you align with their thinking. Show them that they had an impact on you in some beneficial way.
- *Schedule time to network and develop relationships.* Short one-on-one meetings can be a great tool for advancing relationships. Another example is calling several people or a full team together to promote a positive message.
- *Volunteer assistance.* The saying *a person in need is a friend indeed* is oh-so true. When you see a person or group in need of help that you can provide and you relatively quickly rise to the occasion, not only is the other party grateful, but you also feel good about your actions.
- *Keep communications open.* Return texts/messages, phone calls, and e-mails efficiently. Show that you are available and approachable. Show others that you care about them and their needs.
- *Do not blindside.* People don't like surprises, especially if the surprise makes them look bad or can be harmful to their reputation. Always share important information with co-workers in a timely fashion. Especially avoid causing people to look bad publicly.
- *Refrain from blaming others.* Leaders don't blame others; they are too busy solving problems. Blaming others brings no value to the situation and will typically make things worse. When you make others look bad, you typically look bad as well.
- *Keep your commitments.* As we note in an upcoming chapter, making only good commitments and keeping those commitments goes a long way in gaining the respect and

trust of others. It's also a great way to build your professional reputation.

- *Admit when you make a mistake or are wrong.* When you make a mistake, everyone knows it. When you do not admit that mistake, it can cause a barrier to form between you and others. Interestingly, it is common for a person making a mistake and admitting so to be more respected than they were before the mistake was made. People respect honesty and straightforwardness. Caution, however, do not make the same mistake twice or make mistakes often, or your reputation can be tarnished to a point where it will be difficult to repair.

- *Don't talk bad about others.* This behavior can cause a bigger problem than the one currently in front of you. It can also cause a relationship to suffer to a point where recovery becomes less likely.

- *Acknowledge the contributions of others.* Generously give co-workers the recognition they have earned. Who doesn't appreciate being favorably noticed? Most people feel like they are not appreciated as much as they should be, and this recognition can be immensely uplifting.

- *Find the special uniqueness in others.* Everyone has strengths that make them special. Find, recognize, and nurture those attributes. We are all defined more by our strengths than by our weaknesses.

- *Do something daily that can strengthen a relationship.* Pick out a person each day and do something that can build and strengthen the relationship. After weeks or months of doing this, you will find that you have cultivated a vast and rich set of relationships.

- *Be a good role model.* Always play well with others. Constantly ask yourself how you would like the other person to treat you if the situation was reversed.

The more you do for others, whether it be small or large, the more they are likely to be there for you when you need them. Just being a good co-worker can earn their loyalty and support.

Great Relationships Can Yield Great Benefits

If you are thinking that this section feels too contrived and insincere, don't go there. We should be treating others with respect and dignity regardless of the benefits from doing so. It's just that I want you to recognize the great benefits that come from being a model co-worker. Ramping that up a bit more will likely yield even more benefits that, frankly, favor all parties.

Question

Initiating lunch with a co-worker can cause a lunch break to run over the standard lunch duration. Do you see this as a problem?

Answer

Not at all. This is a business lunch. However, it should not harm your commitments the rest of the workday.

Question

If I invite a co-worker to lunch, should I pay?

Answer

In most cases, no. However, if the lunch invite was with a client, and is not frequent, then consider paying. If the lunch invite was with a subordinate and you are a manager, then consider paying.

20. Treat Your Customer as If It Matters

Treat your customer as if it matters—as if the future of your company and your employment rests upon your ability to satisfy your customer on the transaction being performed right now. Treat your customer in a manner that he or she feels special—that shows you care. Every customer interaction should be seen as crucial. The customer can be the person who awaits your deliverable or service and can be either internal or external to your company.

Example

Julie is a project manager. She and her team are building a product for an external customer. The schedule is 10 months, and there are 10 people on the team. Julie works close with the customer and cares that they are satisfied with the development, delivery, and the eventual operation of the product.

She has weekly project meetings and invites a customer rep to attend and ask questions. Once a month, Julie personally meets with the head customer for 30 to 60 minutes. Every three months, she formally administers a survey for the customer to gauge how she is doing and what issues, if any, she needs to address. The survey takes a bit of time, but Julie wants the customer to know that she takes the relationship seriously and wants to ensure it remains strong.

Survey Questions

Here is a list of survey questions. The first seven questions are answered with multiple choice responses of 5-very satisfied, 4-satisfied, 3-neutral, 2-dissatisfied, 1-very dissatisfied, and 0-no comment. The last three questions require written responses.

1. Are you satisfied that you are sufficiently kept informed of project-related information important to you?
2. Are you satisfied with the client–provider relationship?
3. Are you satisfied with the product quality being produced?
4. Are you satisfied with the change control process?
5. Are you satisfied with the management of the budget?
6. Are you satisfied that regulatory issues are under control?
7. Are you satisfied with the success of the project to date?
8. What is your risk forecast in terms of achieving the final delivery date as it is currently scheduled? (3-high risk, 2-medium risk, 1-low risk, and 0-no comment)
9. What are your top three concerns?
10. What are your top three areas of satisfaction?
11. Any additional comments?

Have You Satisfied the Customer?

No matter what product you build or service you provide your customer, always know that it's not about building what *you* think is the right product or providing the right service, it's all about whether you have satisfied the customer, so their needs have been met.

With the care and feeding that Julie provides her customer, there is no doubt that the customer feels special. Of course, in this example, if Julie did *not* intend to be responsive to the customer, she would not have offered to engage so much. As an aside, consider legal counsel before including the external customer rep in project meetings or soliciting the implementation of customer surveys.

Question

I often hear the statement that the client should always come first. Do you agree with this assertion?

Answer

Not always, but almost always. Typically, the client's wishes should come first. However, it is possible that the client's demands are contrary to your company's best interests. In these cases, the client does not come first. The survival of your organization and company does. If your company goes out of business because you chose to satisfy certain client demands, you have created a bigger problem—for both your company and your client's company—than you would have if you had put your own interests first. But, again, the client almost always should come first.

CHAPTER 5

Be Your Best Whole Person

This category reveals the last 4 of the 24 foundational Power Skills:

21. Be a champion for work–life balance
22. Have fun in your work
23. Decide who you choose to be
24. Be a good actor.

21. Be a Champion for Work–Life Balance

Have you ever put off something important or especially fun to you and, in hindsight, you see a pattern emerge of putting such things off—a pattern that is becoming all too common? Join the crowd. Pat McCarty, a retired senior project executive IBM, said:

> *Don't put off the important and fun things until later. Later can have a habit of never arriving.*

There is no right or wrong in how you define your work–life balance. And your needs can change from year to year—sometimes even day to day. You have the right to change your behavior and allocation of your energies at any time. If you frequently demonstrate flexibility, you typically will be rewarded with greater diversity in your life.

Let's Look a Bit Closer

Work–life balance can mean something different to each of us. For purposes of this book, work–life balance is about achieving an acceptable harmony or integration between your work life—or career—and your personal life.

If you have difficulty in juggling the demands of your job and your non-work life, you're not alone. Many people feel like their lives are overbooked and see no relief in sight. Nowadays work–life balance can seem like an unrealistic objective. Technology allows workers to be accessible every hour of every day throughout the year. Work–life balance can seem more elusive than ever.

Not Happy

Studies show that a poor work–life balance can result in unhealthy levels of stress and unhappiness. At risk are your personal relationships, your career, and your development as a person, to name a few. Moreover, too much time spent working has its own problems. You run the risk of burning out and hating your job, maybe even yourself. You wake up one day and realize you're not happy with your life.

Seek a Balance That Suits You

What does matter is that you create a personally meaningful life that helps you feel happy and healthy overall. While balancing work and nonwork life might not be easy early in one's career, figuring it out is necessary to lifelong satisfaction. Almost everyone wishes that they had realized the importance of work–life balance at the beginning of their career. Doing so would have meant less regrets and a more deliberate life. But whatever your age, you can still seize control and drive toward the balance you most desire.

Examples

Of course, whole books are written about work–life balance. But, for our purposes of planting this seed, here are several ideas for your consideration.

Put Yourself First

Take care of yourself. Look out for yourself. Put yourself first. This advice goes against what many of us learned growing up, that is, to put others first. But think about it: Only by putting yourself first, you can be your best so you can give your best to others.

An example is you are on an airplane and the oxygen masks drop due to a potential emergency. You are directed to place the mask on yourself before helping someone in need next to you. You must make sure that you are in a position of strength before you can be your best for all that which comes your way and all those who may depend on you.

Protect Your Private Time

Another example of putting yourself first is protecting your private time. Don't be so quick to sacrifice your private time for other work and personal events. Your private time may be essential for catching your breath, recharging your energy, and reaching a level of understanding and acceptance with yourself and all that is going on around you. If you have serious work–life balance issues, *not* putting yourself first was likely a major cause of the dilemma you now find yourself embroiled in.

"Me" Time

Yet another example is building *me time* into your schedule each day. Studies have shown that a typical workday for most people includes up to two hours of nonproductive time. Let's direct some of that time to *me time*. While planning your week, reserve one to two hours per day of *me time*.

The *me time* should include scheduling one thing you look forward to each day, including on your days off from work. Reserve the item on your calendar and don't view this time as an easy giveaway. Actions that might qualify are reading a book, checking in with a good friend, taking a walk, time for catching up on loose ends, enjoying a 15-minute power nap, or simply being alone.

A little *down time* to recharge your batteries can go a long way, especially on days that are exceptionally hectic. Doing nothing can sometimes be what your health and life need. This recharge time can make the difference between a dreadful day and a satisfying day. Also consider doing something special for yourself at least one evening a week.

Nurturing Diet, Adequate Sleep, and Regular Exercise

Often called *wellness habits*, I rarely see these three actions included in work–life balance discussions. However, if they are ignored, they can have a significant negative impact on your work–life balance. These actions are also all additive in that the sooner you embrace them, the quicker you benefit. The long-term benefit can even add years to your life. But you already know this.

Question

I hear a lot these days about work–life balance. However, I'm a relatively young person with a lot of energy. I don't mind working what many people call excessive overtime. I want to make money while I am young so I can more likely do whatever I choose when I am in my midlife. I also want to make a difference and maybe in the process make a name for myself. Is this a bad thing?

Answer

Of course not. This is your life. I can relate. This was me many years ago. I have personally wrestled with my own work–life balance issues for a large part of my adult life. In my younger adult days, I could easily have been categorized as a workaholic. I liked my job, and the rewards were substantial. However, I was divorced after a 17-year marriage and did not see the break-up coming. I'm not saying that a better work–life balance would have saved the marriage, but a poor work–life balance sure didn't help it any.

As far as some people believe, you only have one life. Use it wisely and thoughtfully. Having passion and unbridled drive can be hugely rewarding, but something may have to give. That something could be, for example, relationships with your existing family circle or building a new family of your own. Just think it through so that years down the road you can look back and feel gratified by the path you chose.

Question

As a leader, do you believe that I have some duty to look out for the work–life balance of my team?

Answer

Yes and no. Yes, in that you need to be up front in what you want in a team member. If you expect their overtime on occasion, they need to know. If you need their undivided and lengthy attention as you are creating a new business, again, they need to know. But also tell them what's in it for them. Some team members don't want to work many extra hours; others are ready with full throttle if they see the benefit for them.

On the flip side, your duty to look out for the work–life balance of your team members is limited. Every team member is different in their wants and needs. They get to choose their trajectory, not you. I believe that the best bosses accommodate employees who would rather restrict their work hours to, say, 40 to 45 hours per week. But they also are willing to accommodate employees who are willing to sacrifice more if the rewards are commensurate with the sacrifice.

22.   Have Fun in Your Work

You spend a huge portion of your waking life at work. For most people, a portion of their work can be difficult, grueling, tedious, challenging, tiring, stressful, exhausting, … need I go on? Just the last sentence alone could be depressing. However, you will be working for most of your life; therefore, you want to find fun in the journey. Finding fun in your job is important at so many levels, including benefiting your productivity, increasing motivation, reducing stress, making your day go faster, and boosting your career enjoyment.

Two Paths

There are two paths you can take to increase your fun at work. You can inject fun activities for you and your co-workers, and you can work on your personal mindset. Let's look at the activities area first.

Fun Activities

For many people, group activities can liven things up a bit. Of course, not everyone enjoys games or public events, so you will want a variety of options. Here are some ideas so you get where I am coming from.

- *Noteworthy achievements.* Take time to celebrate achievements of the team such as meeting a major commitment or completing a huge task.

- *Casual Friday.* Implement casual Friday, when co-workers can dress down, such as with jeans and sneakers.
- *Recreation room.* Create a fun room for taking short breaks with snacks and beverages. Light activities like ping pong, table hockey, and video games can be included.
- *Friendly competition.* Create sporting tournaments after hours where departments and functions can embrace friendly competition with one another. These tournaments can be outdoors, indoors, or virtual.
- *Fun day.* Schedule one day every four to six months when the organization relaxes with outside speakers, personal training topics, and light games.
- *Acknowledge personal moments.* Celebrate employee birthdays and milestones.
- *Happy Hour.* Relax with Happy Hour once a week.

This is a short list and arguably favors non-remote workers. It's best if a team is created to brainstorm ideas and then allow the organization to prioritize the ideas for potential implementation.

Reach Within Yourself

Although activities like those just listed can bring fun to a team or organization, also look within yourself to create a mindset that helps you levitate your own spirits each day. Here are some examples.

- *Embrace gratitude.* Frequently count your many blessings both at work and in your nonwork life.
- *Initiate workplace relationships.* Develop relationships with co-workers, clients, and customers. I'm not talking about being too personal or relationships that necessarily extend outside of work. If that is your aim, fine, but many people are not looking for nonwork personal commitments; they are looking to create good workplace friendships whereby when you enter a meeting and see them, you light up.

- *Help others.* Being generous with your time and being there for a co-worker when needed can be deeply satisfying.
- *Have a personal goal.* Challenge and pace yourself to achieve a personal goal that will benefit the organization such as improving an existing process.
- *Improve your value to your organization.* Fine-tune your technical and Power Skills through onsite or online training.
- *Create a training opportunity.* Develop and instruct a needed class for the organization that not only highlights your skills but also benefits the organization.
- *Own your attitude.* Recognize that changing your attitude to be more positive can change your performance, reputation, and even your life.

Story

Fernando worked for a sizeable company. His office was in the head-quarters building. One day, an executive walked into his office and sat in the guest chair. This was totally unexpected and had never happened before. Fernando had been in several group meetings with the executive but wasn't sure how much he was noticed.

The executive asked Fernando, *Are you having fun?* Fernando was quite intimidated, but thinking quickly on his feet, he replied, *You don't pay me to have fun. You pay me to get the job done.* Whereupon the executive replied, *If you are not having fun, you likely are not doing the best you can.*

Wow! That made a huge impression; so much so, Fernando has counseled countless others on the lesson he learned that day. It is important to find fun in your job. It's on you.

Question

I am at a fork in my work life. I can go one direction and be promoted with promise of good salary increases down the road. But it would require me to take on a role that would not be very exciting for me. Or I can remain on my current path with a job I love with limited opportunity for advancement and smaller pay raises. Any ideas?

Answer

Most people face this choice at several points in their work life. I see it as a good problem to have because you are presented with opportunities. Of course, the answer is highly personal and is based on your short- and long-term goals and vision. I have experienced both forks over my career. As I age, I put a higher premium on enjoying my job and less on advancement and income. Above everything, carefully think through your imagined life on each fork, because your choice will have significant impact on your life for the foreseeable future. I suggest creating the Ben Franklin Pro/Con List to aid in making a determination. It is easily found on the Internet.

23. Decide Who You Choose to Be

Decide who you choose to be, then muster the courage to walk the thought. This book is intended to help you do this.

I don't believe in destiny or fate, but I do believe that things happen for a reason: *because you make them happen or you allow them to happen.* If I thought my life had already been pre-choreographed, then I would not want to get up in the morning. But I believe that each of us does have free will. We easily make many hundreds of choices each day; many small, some not so small.

For example, you choose what time you will get out of bed, what you will have for breakfast and how much of each food, whether the TV is on and, if so, what channel, what you will wear, the route you take to work ... you get the idea. While at work, you make many choices nearly every minute of the day right down to will you immediately respond to that text message to when you will leave work. Although most of us are on autopilot most of the day and we may not obsess with the myriad of choices we are constantly making, these are, nevertheless, true choices that we face.

Our day ends mostly based on the choices we made throughout that day. Our week ends mostly based on the choices we made that week. Our life ends mostly based on the choices we made throughout our life in terms of relationships, health, finances, career, and so on. Therefore, it is important to strive to make careful decisions.

You Are What You Perceive Yourself to Be

Believe that you have significant control over your destiny. Believe that you can make a difference—and you will. Be deliberate when you go to work each day. Decide who you choose to be. Then muster the courage to walk the thought. The following two sentences are likely the most important in this book:

> *You are what you perceive yourself to be.*
> *Your vision becomes your reality.*

Your Performance Is Based on How You Think

You become what you think about all day long. If you think small, so too will be your accomplishments. If you think big, so too will be your accomplishments. Scholars have said these words over the centuries. The most successful leaders have learned to believe in their ability to make things happen—to follow their dreams and transform those dreams into reality.

Live the Life You Most Imagine

It's almost always true that we are our own greatest obstacle to becoming what we truly want to be. If it is important to you, then never, never, never give up. As Henry David Thoreau, the American writer, philosopher, and naturalist, said:

> *If one advances confidently in the direction of his dreams and endeavors to live the life he has imagined, he will meet with a success unexpected in common hours.*

How Can This Book Help You?

This book is exposing you to important Power Skills that can change your career and your life. You can cherry pick the Power Skills you choose to embrace or go all out and seriously consider them all when their use can make a difference.

Optional Exercises

To help you organize your approach to adopting or improving in one or more of the Power Skills, I have optional exercises for you to consider. They are described in detail across Appendices A to C. However, I will give you an overview of the exercises here to whet your appetite. After you have completed this chapter, you can optionally go to Appendix A and begin the exercises.

Briefly, here are the exercises. After reading this chapter, complete a self-assessment questionnaire to gain insight into how proficient you perceive your performance to be in the 24 foundational Power Skills introduced in this chapter. After taking the questionnaire, you will determine your score, and we will discuss what that score might mean for you. Then you can complete another exercise to help you decide the top three Power Skills to focus upon for improvement. Lastly, you can complete an exercise to develop Performance Improvement Plans to help you master the Power Skills you selected.

Although I have found that most readers buy into the notion that all 24 Power Skills have some value, some readers are hesitant to adopt some of these Power Skills based on their life experiences to date and their willingness to stretch themselves.

Although you can review the entire list of Power Skills daily to continuously expose your consciousness to them, having a plan to help focus on those that represent your top three and working that plan daily will help you gain the most benefit from them.

After you have worked your plan to assimilate the top 3 Power Skills into your thinking and actions, you can now revisit the remaining 21 Power Skills (or whatever you view is your number since the first exercise allows you to add your own Power Skills that have special meaning to you) and determine your next three to deliberately work on. You are now on your way to *deciding who you choose to be* and working your way to become that person.

At the end of this chapter, I will remind you of the exercises so you can choose whether to complete them before continuing with the remaining chapters. As I said earlier, the exercises are optional.

Question

You say the exercises are optional. Will I lose important value from this book if I fail to complete the exercises?

Answer

The greatest value of the book is the Power Skills that you are exposed to. As for the exercises, many readers will not have the need, discipline, or time to fully complete the exercises. That's totally okay. But they will offer value for those who need some assistance. By the way, as for the three exercises spread across Appendices A to C, you will gain some value from completing only the first exercise (Appendix A), or the first and second exercises (Appendices A and B), or, of course, all three exercises (Appendices A to C).

Question

You said you did not believe in destiny or fate. How can you really know?

Answer

I can't. However, I find life to be more interesting and hopeful if I believe in free will—that my life mostly plays out based on the choices I make. I see life as an adventure. Moreover, I acknowledge that I cannot control everything that happens in my life, but I can control how I choose to react and carry on. I acknowledge that I am a work in progress, as we all are.

24. Be a Good Actor

The last Power Skill discussed was deciding who you choose to be. Now we need to focus on being a good actor to transform that vision into reality. This will require you to learn to manage your emotions and become deliberate with your actions. As I have said, you become what you think about all day long.

Now that you know the behaviors you most want to mimic, act them out, and do so with passion and conviction. You want to convince your audience. Although this might sound a bit insincere, it's not. This is how you transform your behaviors. You first think about a behavior to adopt. Then you act on that thought to replace an old behavior with the more desirable behavior.

Recall when I introduced *courage* earlier in the chapter. I said to those who did not feel they knew how to acquire courage for themselves, to just fake it! This is an example of what I am talking about here. I have included many thoughts and actions in this book that are often over-looked or intentionally neglected. It's not easy for most people to read all the Power Skills I have discussed and suddenly feel comfortable to adopt and implement them.

Example

Let's look at an example of implementing *be a good actor*.

Take a Ride-Along With Me

As I mentioned earlier, I have conducted over a hundred reviews of troubled projects. When I do this, there are typically 10 to 20 people in the review meeting, sometimes more. Most are members of the project being reviewed, but many are managers or other project managers sitting in to learn tips they can use on their projects. Imagine what it was like for me when I first began reviewing troubled projects.

- I know less than anyone in the room about the project
- My ability to be a quick study (or not) is on display
- My credibility as a project reviewer is on the line
- There is the potential that some people will be embarrassed in front of their peers and management
- I am often working with people who mistakenly think I am out to make them look bad and, therefore, they can withdraw or be defensive

- The clock is ticking, and I must pace to complete the review by a designated time
- And more …

How Do I Cope?

How do I deal with all this pressure and stress? I take it one step at a time. I prepare for the review and let the project members participating in the review know what to expect. I give them homework, the results of which they will present to me while they respond to my many questions.

I look at the Power Skills we have discussed in this book and decide how I can embrace the traits that I may need to rely on the most. Of course, many years ago this book and all its knowledge and wisdom was not in front of me. But I was aware of the importance of many of these Power Skills and diligently worked on adopting them the best I could.

Let's look at some of these Power Skills taken from the list we have already reviewed.

- *Think for yourself.* I need to rely on my analytical skills, not what others say or want me to do.
- *Never avoid necessary confrontation.* If I need to pursue an issue, I will, regardless of the push-back I receive, or the organizational level of the people involved.
- *Don't make it personal or take it personally.* It's not personal. It's just business. I need to remind myself to remain objective and present a positive and thoughtful face.
- *Routinely practice boldness and courage.* I need to present a brave and confident front. I need to boldly pursue any suspect areas of interest.
- *Do not allow what others think about you to be more important than what you think about yourself.* People have a right to their opinions and views. I'm on a mission and I cannot allow myself to be distracted.
- *Live in your present moments.* I must not bring worry or guilt into the review. Don't bring any past or future thoughts from

my personal or professional lives. Remain totally focused on the here and now—totally immersed on this event.

- *Embrace integrity in all that you do.* Always take the high road—do the right thing—following that which is ethical and legal.

- *Trust but verify; inspect what you expect.* Don't trust any assertion in front of me. Seek the truth with questions, stats, artifacts, and history.

- *Treat others as you would like to be treated.* Be respectful at all times. Treat everyone as I would like to be treated if the roles were reversed.

- *Think like a leader.* Remind myself that, as the leader of this review, it's not about the ability of others to lead but my ability to lead despite that which is happening around me.

- *Seek out a mentor.* If I feel that I need a mentor to prep me, then I would do so before the event. Although I never relied on a mentor when I began performing project reviews, a mentor would have been helpful.

- *Evaluate yourself daily.* After the review, I will study the review and identify those things that went well and areas where I could improve. I then factor in this newly acquired information into my next review.

I Know I Can Do This

The more I practiced using these Power Skills, the more comfortable I became with them, and the more they became who I chose to be. After a while, many of the Power Skills became second nature, and I am more at ease. I became what I think about all day long. I believe in myself and know that I can do this.

Answers to Questions Not Addressed Earlier in Chapters 1 to 5

Question

Reading Chapters 1 to 5 was emotionally difficult for me. The 24 Power Skills that were introduced made me realize many of my weaknesses. Any encouraging words for me?

Answer

First and foremost, I respect your willingness to learn the most important Power Skills that define your performance—and your willingness to face the truth about your current performance. All of us have behavior areas where we can improve; you are not alone. Of course, the truth can sometimes hurt but only through knowledge and persistence can we learn and grow.

As you will see in the last section of this chapter, I encourage you to focus on your top three Power Skills to improve—not your top 5 or 10. Let's peel the proverbial onion one layer at a time and not overwhelm ourselves with such a large number of attempted changes that we become ineffective at achieving any of the changes.

Also, don't view your journey in improving your performance as something painful. Instead, be thankful that you have been made aware of Power Skills with which to improve—and seek to find ways to have fun as you selectively but steadfastly improve your performance.

Question

I view that some of the Power Skills would be too stressful for me to effectively implement such as *break the rules occasionally, never avoid necessary confrontation, routinely practice boldness and courage, and trust but verify— inspect what you expect.* This would be too hard for me and out of my comfort zone. Am I wrong to think this way?

Answer

Not necessarily. A great benefit of this section is that it exposes readers to important Power Skills—skills that can be learned through deliberate practice, albeit various degrees of challenge for all of us. My experience is that many readers will work to harness these skills. But there are also some readers that, based on where they are at this point in their personal or professional lives, are willing to expend only so much energy and time to do so. For a person to finish this book and have a much better understanding of what he or she expects from himself or herself is a huge and noteworthy achievement and benefit. It helps make life a bit less complex and stressful as a person learns to feel more comfortable with himself or herself and where they are currently and deliberately heading. Although I believe you can learn these skills, I greatly respect your choices. For a whole bunch of reasons, this may not be an appropriate time in your life to focus on all these Power Skills. I should add that I like you just the way you are. If you choose to grow with some of these Power Skills, that's a bonus for you. But do it because that's what you want.

Question

This chapter discussed 24 foundational Power Skills. In coming up with the list, I assume that there were other Power Skills that were on your mind but did not make the cut for this list. Can you share those Power Skills?

Answer

No. You did not pick up this book to learn about what was not included. In fact, there are many more Power Skills in the next two chapters that relate to teams and interacting with your leaders. When I looked at the relatively short list of Power Skills that did not make this book, I recognized that most of them were reflected in one way or another in the Power Skills that did make the book.

Question

You have mentioned escalations more than once in this chapter. I looked ahead and saw it came up later as well. Where I work, escalation is often a dirty word. Can you expand a bit on this action?

Answer

Escalations are a healthy and essential business tool. Some reasons include, they:

- Provide a check-and-balance mechanism to help ensure that proper action is taken

- Resolve problems early
- Help reduce frustration among project members
- Improve overall productivity by reducing rework that can result from implementing the wrong plan
- Help prioritize work activities
- Encourage employee participation and ownership of problems.

Here are some guidelines for escalating an issue:

- Escalate only after a sincere attempt has been made to resolve the issue with the other party
- The dissenter is typically responsible for escalating the issue
- Initiate the escalation within two workdays of knowing the problem is unresolvable at its current level
- Escalate the problem, not the person
- Always inform your management prior to initiating an escalation if required
- While an escalation is underway, do not stop working the plan of record.

These ideas are further described in my book *Neal Whitten's No-Nonsense Advice for Successful Projects*, published by Management Concepts, 2005.

Question

I did not see *tenacity* or *never give up* in the Power Skills list. What's your views on these Power Skills?

Answer

Never give up briefly came up a time or two. I agree if you want to achieve something important to you, never give up. It's surprising what persistence can do to help you succeed in achieving your goals. Perseverance can level the playing field. It's not about how smart you are; it's what you do with what you have.

I know my own limitations. I'm not the brightest star in the sky but I am very persistent and have great discipline. If you don't have these attributes, the good news is that you can acquire them.

By the way, it's possible that a personal goal might need adjusting from time to time. Sometimes it may be time to give up and redirect your energies. Be open to reassessing a goal's importance and achievability so you remain reasonably realistic. However, I should add if you do quit short of your goals, you will never know what you might have become.

Question

I didn't see anything about one's ego in the list of foundational Power Skills. Can you say something about ego?

Answer

Stroking your ego can be detrimental. But since you brought the topic up, let's briefly pay ego a visit.

Do not bring your ego to work … ever. Check it at the proverbial doorstep before entering. It's never about you. It's about the project, the sponsor, the client, the team, the company, making your boss look good (oh yes, you read correctly; your job includes making your boss look good which we will address in an upcoming chapter), and about a bunch of other objectives.

If you bring your ego to work, it will only trip you up. An overactive ego can get in the way of making sound judgments, establishing and maintaining good working relationships, and learning and growing from our mistakes. You will see your effectiveness and reputation grow if you keep your ego at bay.

Let's look at some downsides to practicing an oversized ego.

- Reluctance to praise co-workers
- Excessively seeks attention
- Quick to find fault with others
- Frequently too defensive
- Tendency to pretend to know more than they do

- Delivers the truth in a hurtful manner
- Not accepting accountability
- Talks down to others
- Damages reputations with gossip
- Promotes self-importance
- Plagued with jealousy
- Practices self-pity
- Thinks they are better than others
- Seeks instant gratification at the expense of others
- Less friendships.

Ouch! This is a nasty list, yet it could be much longer. An interesting sidebar of those who practice a large ego is that their behavior is likely causing the opposite affect than what they are seeking. It is causing people around them to have less admiration, respect, and trust for them. People would rather not be in their presence or associated with them. Would you want to be around a person who behaves in the manner revealed in the above list? Of course not. Neither would I.

Look, we all have an ego. And most of us work at keeping it at bay so it doesn't interfere with who we wish to be and who we want others to see us as. But we may trip up occasionally. That's okay if we learn from the experience and make restitution, if applicable, with the results of that behavior. For example, if we inappropriately hurt someone, then apologize.

I'm often asked if an exaggerated ego will interfere with a person being a leader? It is possible to qualify as a leader and still exercise a huge ego. You can still achieve big things. However, most people will not want to work with you or around you. The environment will be too toxic and uncomfortable. Moreover, people will not see you as trustworthy. The result is that your job will become more difficult, and you become less effective.

Refocus energy that you might spend feeding a high ego with building relationships and getting the work done that you are tasked with. The less approval you demand from others, the more you are likely to receive.

Question

I could not find any mention of taking responsibility for your own performance and career. Was this an oversight?

Answer

No. There were Power Skills that arguably could be considered lightly touching on this such as *think for yourself, decide who you choose to be,* and *evaluate yourself daily.* But you are correct, the topic was not specifically introduced. However, I would like to take this opportunity to say a few words on this.

You are responsible, of course, for your performance and career. Don't abdicate that responsibility to your boss, your company, or anyone else. But do take advantage of the benefit that your boss can provide you in areas such as training, coaching, and opportunities. As a sidebar, freely toot your own horn to your boss; let him or her know about your noteworthy deeds. Your boss wants to know and needs to know this information while evaluating your performance and helping you chart a course for your career; however, don't focus on horn tooting to co-workers—no one else wants to know or cares. (More on tooting your own horn in an upcoming chapter.)

Question

During the Introduction, you suggested that the Power Skills are also for your nonwork life. Is it really a good idea to apply all these Power Skills outside of work? Won't doing so bring too much tension and stress?

Answer

Many of the Power Skills will serve you just fine in your personal life, such as *live in your present moments, embrace integrity in all that you do, treat others as you would like to be treated,* and *be a champion for work–life balance.* Some Power Skills mostly focus on the work environment, such as *mind your own business first, trust but verify—inspect what you expect, treat all project members equally,* and *have fun in your work.* However, my view is that one's personal life tends to be less aggressive and more laid back and relaxed than the work life. Therefore, less attention will likely be directed to Power Skills such as *break the rules occasionally, never avoid necessary confrontation, routinely practice boldness and courage,* and *evaluate yourself daily.* Most importantly, it is up to you and your chosen lifestyle to decide which Power Skills you will embrace in your personal life.

List of Foundational Power Skills

Here is a summary list of the 24 foundational Power Skills we have just discussed. For those who deliberately embrace them, your career and life can dramatically benefit.

Printable Copy

You can obtain a printable copy of the summary list by visiting my website at:

nealwhittengroup.com/powerskills/

Be Your Own Bold Self

1. *Break the rules occasionally.* Oftentimes, you will find that following conventional rules will not effectively or efficiently solve an issue.
2. *Never avoid necessary confrontation.* Always give problems the sense of urgency and importance they deserve.
3. *Routinely practice boldness and courage to be a consistently effective leader.* Your behavior drives your success.
4. *Think for yourself.* Challenge tradition, authority, and the status quo in a professional and mature manner. Routinely question your own behaviors and actions.
5. *Do not allow what others think about you to be more important than what you think about yourself.* Listen for helpful snippets but remain in control of you.

Take Care of Current Business

6. *Manage daily to your top three priorities.* They define your value and contributions and, ultimately, your career.

7. *Mind your own business first.* Behave as if you own the business and your business is defined by your domain of responsibility.

8. *Live in your present moments.* Don't dwell on yesterday. Admit mistakes, learn from them, apply those lessons going forward ... and move on. And don't worry about the future. Plan for it but live fully in the now.

9. *Don't make it personal or take it personally.* It's all about what's best for business.

10. *Embrace integrity in all that you do.* Listen to your inner voice and treat it as the wise and trusted friend it is.

Be a Role Model by Your Leadership

11. *Think like a leader.* It's not about the ability of those around you to lead; it's about your ability to lead, regardless of what is happening around you.

12. *Treat others as you would like to be treated.* You will be remembered and revered for how you made others feel.

13. *Trust but verify; inspect what you expect.* Strive to build trust among project stakeholders, but insist on metrics, checks and balances, and other tools to ensure outcomes are being met.

14. *Understand and practice empowerment.* Understand your job, take ownership of it, and do whatever is necessary—within legal and ethical parameters—to accomplish it.

15. *Treat all project members equally.* All project members, regardless of where they come from or to whom they report, must be held accountable for their commitments.

16. *Promote diversity, equity, and inclusivity.* Benefits include employees are more engaged, feel more appreciated and respected, and their commitment, trust, and morale increase. However, DEI must be implemented fairly and justly.

Use Constructive Interactions to Improve

17. *Seek out a mentor.* We can learn far more and far faster when we can draw strength from those who have gone before us.

18. *Evaluate yourself daily.* As professionals, self-assessments of our actions are essential for our continued growth, professional maturity, and effectiveness.

19. *Promote mutual relationships.* When your relationships are viewed as strong, more can get done in less time, with less stress, with greater productivity, and you probably like your job more.

20. *Treat your customer as if it matters …* as if the future of your company and your employment rests upon your ability to satisfy your customer on the transaction being performed right now.

Be Your Best Whole Person

21. *Be a Champion for Work–Life Balance.* Almost everyone wishes they had realized the importance of work–life balance sooner rather than later. Doing so can mean less regrets and a more deliberate life. But whatever your age, you can still seize control and drive toward the balance you most desire.

22. *Have fun in your work.* Finding fun in your job is important at so many levels from benefiting your productivity, increasing motivation, reducing stress, making your day go faster, and boosting your career enjoyment.

23. *Decide who you choose to be.* This book is exposing you to important Power Skills that can change your career and your life. You can cherry pick the Power Skills you choose to embrace or go all out and seriously consider them all when their use can make a difference.

24. *Be a good actor.* Continuously work at being the person you choose to be. You first identify a Power Skill to adopt. Then you act on that thought to replace an old behavior with the more desirable behavior.

Exercises

I said I would remind you at the end of this chapter about the exercises. Here we are.

These exercises can help you accomplish three goals:

1. Gain insight into how proficient you perceive your performance to be in the 24 foundational Power Skills introduced in this chapter
2. Determine your top three Power Skills with which to focus
3. Create a Performance Improvement Plan for each of these three Power Skills. These plans can give you structure on your journey to mastering these Power Skills.

These exercises are optional, extra credit if you will. However, do not overlook the benefit you can derive from intentionally laser-focusing on three (or less) Power Skills with the intent of putting them into practice.

To conduct the first exercise, go to *Appendix A. Questionnaire for Self-Assessing Your Foundational Power Skills*. After performing this exercise, you will be directed to *Appendix B. Determine Top Three Power Skills of Importance to You*. Lastly, you will be directed to *Appendix C. Performance Improvement Plans* where you will be coached on how to create the plans.

When you are ready, move on to the next section.

SECTION 2

Power Skills for a Team

Shared Values

As a team member, you need to know the Power Skills expected of you that will help you to perform at your best. If you are a team leader, you need your team members to know the Power Skills that you expect from them, that they should expect from one another, and from you so the team can perform at its best.

If you were building a team and could handpick its members, what are the key attributes you would look for in each member? What are the behaviors and actions necessary for them to perform at their best and the team to perform at its best? In other words, what Power Skills make a team member valuable?

Team members cannot be expected to already know or practice these Power Skills. These behaviors and actions must be revealed as the team is forming and reinforced throughout the project. Praise should generously be bestowed on those members who demonstrate these tenets notably. But members not performing to an acceptable level will need coaching and nurturing so that they can become proficient as well.

This chapter will use both the terms *project member* and *team member* interchangeably. I have chosen to do so because of the general acceptance of both these terms in many work environments.

This section presents 15 of the most important behaviors—Power Skills—of the desired project member. The 15 Power Skills are divided into two categories:

- Take accountability for your responsibilities
- Support the team by your personal behaviors.

Each of the 15 behaviors is presented in three segments. The first segment describes the behavior. The next segment offers an example to show the behavior being applied. The last segment wraps up with a brief discussion of the example and any closing thoughts about the behavior.

Before we proceed, it's important to say that the foundational Power Skills presented in the preceding chapter are for everyone—including team members. This chapter will not duplicate any of those Power Skills. Instead, it will present additional Power Skills that have special relevance to members that are working as a team. Think of these Power Skills as a set of core values—shared values—that help a team's members work most proficiently for the benefit of the team.

The Power Skills are listed in no particular order. Let's now look at the first of the two chapters that describe the Power Skills for a team.

CHAPTER 6

Take Accountability for Your Responsibilities

This category reveals the first 7 of the 15 Power Skills for a team:

1. Be truthful
2. Be reliable
3. Demonstrate personal initiative
4. Ask for help
5. Practice being proactive
6. Focus on solutions
7. Practice continuous improvement.

1. Be Truthful

Be truthful and timely when revealing your progress and issues. When you make a mistake, admit it, and take accountability. When you are faced with making a commitment, make only good commitments.

Example

Oscar is a project member. Several times a week he must provide status on his portion of the project. Oscar always gives a truthful accounting of his status and problems. He has learned that being truthful, even about bad news like being late toward a commitment, allows him and the project manager to focus on recovery and potential mitigation with other stakeholders; otherwise, problems can drift and fester further.

Oscar never has to be coaxed to give truthful and timely status nor does he ever want to be the weak link on the team that can arise by holding back important information. Oscar is also truthful about mistakes that he makes if others can benefit by knowing about them. When asked to make a commitment, Oscar is truthful about only making good commitments. The commitments may be aggressive, but they are always believed to be achievable.

Discussion

Oscar clearly sees the value both to him and his team in being truthful about making only good commitments as well as providing accurate and timely status on those commitments. Although it's never fun to give bad news, Oscar also recognizes the value of providing the bad news both accurately and timely. The truth is essential for all team members if the team is to function at its peak.

Question

Don't you think that holding back from the truth until you are 100 percent sure whether you can recover on your own is best? Otherwise, you raise alarms that may not have been necessary.

Answer

Better to raise an alarm and alert the affected parties, than risk holding back which could cause harm to the team or project. If you owned the company, how would you want your employees to interact to best support the success of the business?

2.   Be Reliable

Be reliable and meet your commitments. Always do what you say you are going to do and when you said you would do it. A team is only as strong as its weakest link—don't be a weak leak. Produce quality work consistently. Demonstrate personal pride in fulfilling your commitments.

Example

Deidra is a project member. She is accountable for about a dozen activities in the project plan. She also has about a dozen open action items assigned to her at any point in time. Deidra prides herself in almost always making her commitments whether they are short-term such as most commitments associated with action items or longer term such as activities in the project plan.

Deidra works in a highly dynamic environment and occasionally finds her workload to be excessive and a commitment must slip. When this happens, Deidra always works on a mitigation plan with the stakeholders who have a dependency on the commitments that are in jeopardy, as well as her project manager. She makes sure that they have heard about a commitment slip from her before they hear about it from someone else or in a routine project tracking meeting. Deidra is serious about her deliverables being at an acceptable level of quality and does not sacrifice quality in order to achieve a scheduled commitment.

Discussion

Deidra appears to be highly reliable both in meeting time commitments and meeting quality commitments. When a commitment is in jeopardy, Deidra takes the initiative to work with dependent stakeholders to best address the issue. No one can always meet every commitment they have made, but it appears Deidra can be relied upon to responsibly address potentially late commitments.

Notice in this example that Deidra did not wait for her project manager or manager to tell her what to do if a commitment looks like it may be in jeopardy. She took the initiative to communicate and resolve the issue relatively quickly. Your reputation for being reliable is earned one commitment at a time.

Question

What should I do if I am assigned to a project before I fully understand the magnitude of the new commitment, and other duties prohibit me from fulfilling the expected commitment?

Answer

Be truthful. Work with your project manager to negotiate an acceptable solution. If you are unable to resolve the issue, then include your manager in the discussion. Your manager likely has a far broader set of options that he or she might be able to suggest. Never stick your head in the sand and imply a commitment that you suspect you cannot fulfill.

3.   Demonstrate Personal Initiative

Practice personal initiative when appropriate. Require minimal leadership. Ensure you understand your assignment and domain of responsibility. If you are unsure about taking an action, then seek appropriate counsel. Make things happen.

Example

Enrique is a project member and has been assigned to the project since its inception. Three months into the project, there are over 30 members, and that number is growing by the week. There are many questions floating about that relate to each member's domain of responsibility. In other words, Enrique sees members tripping over one another not sure of the reaches and limits of their duties.

Enrique sees this situation as a major obstacle to his personal performance, not to mention the project's success. He decides to define what he believes is his domain of responsibility—those activities, deliverables, and duties with which he will be held accountable. He then meets with both his manager and the project manager to discuss his perspective. A lively and important discussion ensues that not only helps Enrique nail down his domain of responsibility but provides insights for the project manager to ensure that other members of the project are clearly aware of their domains of responsibility as well. This meeting inspired the project manager to work with key members across the project to clarify their responsibilities.

Discussion

We often hear that one person cannot make a big difference. Of course, that view is not true as Enrique demonstrated. Because of his personal initiative, he not only was able to nail down his own domain of responsibility, but he also inspired the project manager to focus on a prevailing problem that went far beyond just Enrique. Think about how great a team can be if each member was to demonstrate the personal initiative that Enrique had.

Question

It seems that both Enrique's manager and his project manager were remiss in doing their jobs: Making clear in the beginning what Enrique's domain of responsibility was. Why should Enrique have to do this?

Answer

You are correct that Enrique's manager and his project manager each had a role in defining Enrique's job—also called domain of responsibility. But if Enrique took no initiative to resolve this dilemma, then he would become part of the problem as well as have his own performance suffer. He wasn't content in just knowing that these two leaders had weakly done their jobs; as a mature professional, he took the initiative to get this resolved.

4. Ask for Help

In the increasingly complex and competitive world, we are asked to do more with less. All of us, if we are truly stretching ourselves, will be overwhelmed occasionally. Often, asking for help is the right behavior to embrace. Asking for help is a sign of strength, not weakness. Doing so can not only increase your personal value but can be a big benefit to your team. As a side benefit, many times you will find that the people you go to for help may feel honored by your recognition that they can help you.

Example

Shalena is relatively new to the team. She has been assigned what she believes is a lot of work and knows it will be a stretch for her to complete her assignments on time. Shalena runs into an obstacle and is not certain of the best approach to take. She visits her team leader and reveals her problem as well as several potential solutions. Putting their heads together, Shalena eventually walks away with what she now believes to be the best approach.

Discussion

Shalena did well. She was aware that she has little or no time to waste. When she ran into an obstacle, she considered several options and decided to get another opinion. Working closely with her team leader, she was able to walk away from the meeting with the confidence that she was making the decision that was in the best business interest of the team.

Notice that Shalena went to her team leader with several potential solutions instead of expecting her team leader to solve her problem. The team leader's respect for Shalena likely strengthened because of Shalena's actions. If you are not asking for help when you need it, you become part of the problem.

Question

Aren't you concerned that team members may abuse asking others for help?

Answer

Almost all people want to do the right thing and will use good judgment in asking for help. In the infrequent cases, where someone has performance issues, is in the wrong job, or is a slacker looking for others to carry them, those are issues that need to be addressed with his or her team leader and manager.

Question

Why are team members often reluctant to ask for help?

Answer

There are many reasons, of course. It could be pride. It could be the assumption that they will look bad, perhaps incompetent. It could be that a person must ask for help from someone younger in age or lower in job level. It could be bashfulness or a cultural thing. However, none of these reasons is an acceptable excuse for not asking for help! A mature professional will ask for help rather than harm the team or project.

5.   Practice Being Proactive

Don't just focus on the task at hand, also look at the tasks coming up to help ensure you and your team's readiness. Practice being proactive and make it a standard practice to think one or more steps ahead.

Example

Bonnie is a team member. She has a weak reputation for meeting her commitments and would like to improve her commitment-meeting track record. She studied the commitments she had made over the past several years looking for tips that can help her improve. Although many factors were at play, one factor stood out like a shiny object among a bland backdrop: *being proactive.*

Bonnie discovered that when she spent little or no time focusing early on the upcoming activities, she was often underprepared. This situation frequently caused delays that could have been avoided by thinking ahead and working earlier with others with whom she had a dependency. Consequently, Bonnie now includes in her routine status reports not just what she recently accomplished and her current progress but also reporting preparation work required within a 30-day outlook.

Discussion

The big message here is to not overlook the importance of practicing being proactive; that is, planning ahead rather than having to react to an underplanned activity. In Bonnie's case, she discovered for herself the benefits of doing so and institutionalized a technique in her routine status reports to think about and plan more for the near-term future.

Question

My workday is very busy. I hardly have time to do my base job. I don't see how I can add planning well ahead to my jammed-busy schedule. Comments?

Answer

Planning is not performing extra credit. Your job includes planning ahead. If you cannot find the time to do so, then you might be overcommitted. In this case, you need to discuss your need for relief with your team leader and/or manager. This situation requires your action to address.

6. Focus on Solutions

The most professionally mature members do not engage in finger-pointing and the blame game. Instead, they are busy focusing on solving issues and moving forward. Be a problem solver. Focus on solutions. Recognize that we all make mistakes and that we need to learn from them and not repeat the same mistakes.

Example

Aimee joins a 12-month project 6 months after it has started. She is replacing a team member who has left the project. That team member left a big mess for Aimee. Commitments were being missed, quality was low, his planning was in disarray, and his assigned activities were now in the project's critical path. Aimee saw all this as an opportunity.

Aimee never resorted to the blame game. For whatever reason, her predecessor was failing. We all make mistakes from time to time but highlighting her predecessor's troubles and continually restating them add no value whatsoever to the project. Instead, Aimee focused on solutions and what she needed to do.

As an aside, Aimee preferred to take on a portion of a project that was in trouble than to have started at the beginning of the project. Not only can Aimee learn from her predecessor's mistakes, but she can also feel a great sense of accomplishment as she turns around a troubled piece of the project.

Discussion

Aimee performed like a true professional: focusing on solutions, not stuck in the blame game. The more energy one uses on solving versus blaming, the faster forward progress can be achieved. As a side benefit, a person's reputation can also benefit.

Question

When a team member causes problems for the team, he or she should be called out on it. Why should anyone get a free pass?

Answer

Usually when a team member messes up, everyone knows it. Focusing on punishing that person does nothing to solve the problem and move on. We all mess up from time to time. Cut others some slack here. If the mess up is frequent, then the team leader and manager need to focus on addressing the ongoing performance problem.

7.   Practice Continuous Improvement

Seek ways to continually improve your skills as well as the processes and procedures that you and your team engage in. Become and remain the subject matter expert in your chosen domain. Be open and accepting to constructive criticism. Don't just correct a problem; seek to correct the process that allowed the problem to occur. Encourage feedback on your performance. Adapt to change.

Example

Cody is a project member. He cares about being better today than he was yesterday and still better tomorrow than he is today. In his search for continuous improvement, here is a technique he has adopted. Cody reports on his work status each week to his project manager and his manager. After doing so, he closely examines his performance the past week and seeks to identify any actions that he could have taken that would have improved his performance. He then identifies ways how that information can improve his performance going forward.

Another practice that Cody has taken up is visiting his manager once a month and requesting an on-the-spot performance rating based on what his manager experienced about Cody the past month. This practice not only helps Cody learn ways to improve his performance, but he also learns behaviors that he wants to repeat. Another benefit is that he will likely not be surprised with his performance evaluation rating the next time his official review occurs. An aside is that this action clearly sends the message to his boss that Cody is always searching for how he can be a more valuable employee.

Discussion

Cody clearly is committed to continuous improvement. Continuous improvement is essential for building better products and providing better services. That improvement begins with each of us and extends to teams, projects, organizations, and companies. If you are not continuously growing, then you are setting yourself and your team up to be weakly competitive in this increasingly competitive world.

Question

Should I inform my manager of all the areas I have continuously improved in during my performance period?

Answer

I wouldn't. I respect your focus on improvement. Your manager should know how sincere you are to continuously improve your performance. But be careful highlighting your flaws that you are correcting. Your manager likely did not know about most of them. Nor does your manager have the time to spend on that level of detail.

CHAPTER 7

Support the Team by Your Personal Behaviors

This category reveals the last 8 of the 15 Power Skills for a team:

8. Fully participate
9. Share knowledge
10. Maintain a positive attitude
11. Be willing to compromise
12. Support the ideas of others
13. Give praise to others
14. Advocate a sense of humor
15. Promote team success.

8. Fully Participate

The first behavior is *fully participate*. Voluntarily speak up in meetings and get-togethers. Contribute ideas, even if they may be unconventional—many times thinking out of the box brings the team to the best solution. Your opinion is important and can help identify or move an issue closer to resolution. Be forthcoming to both ask and answer questions.

Example

Louis is a team leader whose team is faced with a challenging problem. Unless the problem can be creatively resolved, the team's upcoming major milestone will likely be missed by at least four weeks. Louis calls a meeting of a half dozen team members in hopes of coming up with an innovative solution. Sergio, a meeting attendee, has an idea and shares it with the group. The idea seems promising at first but after some discussion, the idea is abandoned.

Ideas from other team members surface and are discussed. Sergio actively participates in the discussions—asking questions and seriously considering the ideas. Sergio floats another idea—albeit somewhat unconventional. The idea gains support and is eventually adopted, allowing the upcoming major milestone to complete on schedule.

Discussion

Sergio appeared to be a strong participator. He was forthcoming with his own ideas as well as asking questions and seriously considering the ideas of his peers. In this case, Sergio had proposed the idea that, after some group discussion and perhaps refinement, solved the issue. However, regardless of whose idea was adopted, Sergio's active participation helped the meeting be more productive and to reach its intended objective. By the way, a team is only as effective as its members' contributions.

Question

Do you believe that the team leader has the duty to encourage full participation from the meeting attendees?

Answer

Yes, but responsibly. No berating or put downs or being judgmental. If a member is especially quiet or reserved, occasionally ask for his opinion in the matter at hand. I find that being quiet does not necessarily mean that a person is ill-informed or without an opinion. A goal is to eventually have all members comfortable in speaking up when they have something to add.

9.   Share Knowledge

Yes, knowledge is power. But the best performers give it away—they don't hoard it. They recognize the benefit of sharing knowledge in strengthening the team and raising their own value and reputation in the process.

Example

Jitka was hired into the organization about six months ago. At that time, she also began work as a project member of a new project that is expected to be about a year in duration. For the first month or two, Jitka often sought help from others in getting on board and up to speed—help for which she was most grateful. Jitka is a relatively fast learner and after two months or so, she required little help from others. Instead, she found herself as the go-to person for many of her co-workers.

Jitka was aware of the saying *knowledge is power* and also aware that people tended to one extreme or the other: share knowledge or don't share knowledge. Jitka decided to behave as she would want her employees to behave if she owned the company: Share knowledge so that we all can learn and grow from one another and, in the process, move the business forward. By the time the project ended, Jitka was easily one of the most valuable people on the project. She had earned a great reputation for sharing her knowledge and helping others.

Discussion

Jitka got it right. Your leaders want and need employees and project members who freely give knowledge to others. This great business practice not only helps promote the success of the project, organization, and company but is invaluable to your own reputation and career.

Question

I have a concern that the more knowledge I share with others the less competitive I become and the more competitive my co-workers become. What are your thoughts on this?

Answer

As I mentioned earlier, look at this situation from the perspective of owning the company. How would you want your employees to interact to best support the success of the business? It's a no-brainer; you would want them to share their knowledge.

My view is that the person who has a reputation for sharing knowledge is likely well respected and seen as a role model for others. Even though your co-workers are gaining knowledge, you also are always gaining knowledge. But it's not just about knowledge; it's also about attitude and the willingness to look out for your team.

10.   Maintain a Positive Attitude

Adopt a can-do spirit, and a positive attitude. Be thankful for and even look forward to the challenges and opportunities before you. Place a constructive view on issues—seek out the sun during cloudy and stormy moments. Don't take or make things personal.

Example

Tatiana is a team member. A co-worker disagrees with Tatiana on an issue and escalates the issue to Tatiana's manager after attempting to resolve the issue with Tatiana. Tatiana loses the escalation. Both during and after the escalation meeting, Tatiana maintains a positive attitude and does not take it personally that a co-worker has escalated an issue to her manager. Tatiana realizes that escalations are a good business tool for sorting out issues and ensuring that the best business solutions are achieved.

In another example, Tatiana's team leader is out of the office for two weeks. Tatiana has been asked to cover for him. Although her workload was full without this additional assignment, she is flattered to have this opportunity. Every day of the two weeks sees team members contacting her regarding issues, questions, and invites to meetings. She remains enthused, is having a lot of fun, and even learning some things in the process.

Tatiana finds that she must work overtime but feels that that is a small price to pay for the opportunity to help her team leader, the team members, as well as the opportunity to expand her experience. When Tatiana attends a meeting, she is determined to build a reputation as being viewed as a net positive in the meeting rather than a net negative.

Discussion

Let's discuss the two examples. Tatiana maintained a great attitude in both examples. In the first example, she viewed the escalation in the light that it should be: Not personal but an important business tool. Problems are attacked, not people.

In the second example, Tatiana was honored to be chosen as the backup team leader. She saw every problem that surfaced over the two weeks as opportunities, not obstacles, and embraced the challenges. Tatiana's actions caused her to be an inspiration—a role model—to those she worked with.

Question

How will having a positive attitude help me?

Answer

There is a saying, *you can change your life by changing your attitude.* Everyone wants to work around people with great attitudes. No one wants to be around party poopers. Having a good attitude helps us see life as a great opportunity—an adventure—that we are blessed to experience.

We all have our obstacles and burdens, but these are not what define us. We are, instead, defined by our dreams and hopes and the actions we take to achieve them. A person's greatest obstacle is almost always himself or herself. Dare to be different. Dare to be bold. Dare to reach for your dreams, despite everything that is going on around you.

Question

How can I maintain a positive attitude when I work around negative people?

Answer

Don't allow others to define you. You choose your own attitude; nobody chooses it for you. A positive attitude can be contagious but, of course, so can a negative one. People will look forward to being around and working with you if you consistently demonstrate a positive attitude.

If others' negative behavior is undermining your ability to achieve your commitments, then you must act. However, if the person with the negative attitude has no influence within your domain of responsibility, then you can choose to do nothing. If you are around the person frequently, you may choose to encourage a change in that person's attitude or at least try to better understand what is behind it, but that is your choice.

John C. Maxwell, a leadership expert, fittingly said, *Attitude: It is our best friend or our worst enemy.*

11. Be Willing to Compromise

Compromising on an issue is often required to resolve it. Everyone can't always have it their way. Compromising can also spread goodwill and strengthen relationships. Just make sure that the compromise is something the business can live with. If there is serious harm to the business, then work harder to protect the business—even considering escalating the issue to higher leadership. However, the good news is that there is usually more than one outcome that is satisfactory, albeit it may need to be creative.

Example

Mike and Stephanie are members of the same team. Mike needs assistance from Stephanie with her special skills for him to meet his team commitments. But Stephanie is already working overtime and has no free time to accommodate Mike's needs. If Mike cannot get the help he needs, then the entire team will suffer from his slipped schedules.

Stephanie suggests including the team leader, Tom, in the discussion. Tom has good ideas and has access to other people's resources on the team. Tom was able to resolve the issue by temporarily assigning two other team members to take on some of Stephanie's work while Stephanie is freed up to help Mike.

Discussion

Notice everyone is sincere about solving the issue. They want the team to be successful. No one is throwing their hands up and acting as if there is no way to solve this issue. Stephanie's suggestion to get Tom on board with the problem was her way of demonstrating that there must be some compromising that can happen across the team to solve the issue that she and Mike were unable to resolve on their own. Although the bulk of the compromising came from the team leader and reassigning his team's resources, this solution may not have occurred had Stephanie not suggested looking at the bigger picture outside of just her and Mike.

Question

I work with several co-workers who see compromising as an admission that their solution was weak. Their dug-in position is that it becomes their way or the highway. Comments?

Answer

It's not personal, it's business. If you cannot convince them to work with you and you believe that the position on the table is not in the business' best interest, then escalate the issue higher. Don't be a party to bad compromises or you become part of the problem.

12.   Support the Ideas of Others

Be willing to listen to and be open to the ideas of others. When a decision is appropriately made, fully support that decision even if it was different from what you would have preferred. Show your willingness to cooperate with others. Your support is a form of honoring your team members.

Example

Sunil is a project member on a team of about a dozen members. The project is challenging in terms of schedule, technology, complexity, and funding. Most of the team spends an appreciable amount of their time in work meetings trying to find the most productive path forward. There are many creative and talented minds in these meetings.

Sunil thoughtfully listens to the ideas and does his best to consider constructively and open-mindedly each idea. He asks questions—sometimes promoting his own ideas—but always searching for the best business outcome. In most cases, the ideas that become adopted are not his own—although he may have improved upon some of them.

Sunil believes that what's important is not so much his ability to promote and sell his own ideas but to recognize and support the best ideas—no matter where they may come from. He believes that if everyone thinks this way, the collective value of the whole team far surpasses the sum of the value of each team member individually.

Discussion

Sunil is correct in his philosophy that *the whole is worth more than the sum of its parts*. This thinking helps ensure that the best ideas emerge. Furthermore, the best ideas must also be fairly considered with no bias for where the ideas came from. We must get past the *me* and focus on the *we*.

Question

I'm all for supporting the ideas of others if those ideas have merit. But many do not. Comments?

Answer

An original idea may be weak. But that doesn't mean it doesn't have potential with some modifications. Almost all ideas have some merit as a starting point. Keep your mind open and seek to evolve a weak idea into a noteworthy idea by adding your creative juices to the mix.

13.   Give Praise to Others

Recognize the contributions of others and give credit where it is due. Support others in experiencing the appreciation that they have earned.

Example

Stan received some needed help from a co-worker, Reilly. He acknowledged the help to his manager who is also Reilly's manager—during a weekly team meeting. In another weekly team meeting, Stan recognized Tinsley for something Tinsley had done that apparently had gone unnoticed but was a big help to the team. In yet another incident a short time later, another co-worker, Talon, received an award. The first chance Stan had, he congratulated Talon on his award.

Stan believes that people are typically not recognized and appreciated as much as they could or should be. He knows how much it means to him when someone goes out of their way to appreciate some deed he has done, and he wants to share those special moments when they surface for others.

Discussion

What can we learn here? Stan appears to do a great job of recognizing his peers for their achievements. If you were a peer at the receiving end of Stan's praise, wouldn't you love it? Stan's correct in thinking that no one is ever appreciated as much as they feel is deserved. However, don't let that stop you from praising others just as you would like others to praise you during those special moments. Such behavior can be infectious and help promote goodwill across a team.

Question

Why should I praise others when they do a good deed or have earned recognition for some noteworthy thing they did when I infrequently receive praise and recognition for the good things I do?

Answer

Really? You don't know why? It's called professional maturity. It's taking the high road. It's contributing to building good relationships and goodwill. It's the decent thing to do. It also can encourage others to be more vocal about the good deeds of their co-workers—including your good deeds.

By the way, when praise does come your way, savor that moment—it may not last long.

14.   Advocate a Sense of Humor

Your job is serious business but let's not overlook the value of humor to lighten our load. Be willing to laugh at yourself and some of the situations you will find yourself in. Work at lifting the team's spirit and morale. As I stated in an earlier chapter, if you are not having fun, you are not giving your best.

Example

Jack is a member of a two-year project. He has recommended that the project members take a half-day every six months to celebrate their accomplishments and just kick back and have some fun. One activity of the half-day event would be gifting selected members with gag gifts intended to be humorous in the guise of awards for their accomplishments to date.

For example, Bob provides remarkably high quality for his deliverables. The award proposed for Bob is a paper plate that has been spray painted with gold paint on both sides of the plate. The implication is that Bob's quality is so high that he even manages to gold plate the plate's underside even though it will never be seen or used.

Another example is Carol who has an accounting background. Her gag gift would be a can of beans because she seems the happiest when she has some beans to count.

Paco, who is the liaison between the marketing and development groups, would be gifted two bottles, one of oil and the other of vinegar, as practice for successfully mixing the two groups.

Discussion

Jack is looking to create an event for everyone on the project to enjoy and have some fun—something that can help lift the team's spirits. One of his goals is to infuse some humor into the workplace in a manner that also recognizes the value and importance of various project members.

The team atmosphere can be a whole lot more inviting if we can look at the light side of what we do. If you are not very creative at sharing tasteful and funny situations, at least enjoy and support those around you who do have those talents. And don't overlook self-deprecating humor where you may have messed up somewhere and instead of being defensive, turn the situation around with good-natured humor that acknowledges you goofed.

Question

The example shown was related to inserting humor into a half-day get-together that happened only twice a year. But what about injecting some light-heartedness—some humor—into my workday. Is this okay in a professional work environment?

Answer

Yes, assuming it is in good taste and at an appropriate moment. A well-timed bit of humor is often sorely needed. All too often we fail to loosen up and find the humor in ourselves and our situation.

How terribly depressing for team members to resist expressing the lighter side of the daily problems they face. Displaying a sense of humor also helps you to remain cool under pressure and keep problems in perspective. Humor has been shown to preserve the health of individuals; it also can promote the health of a project or organization.

15. Promote Team Success

See yourself as there to serve your team to the best of your ability. Show that you care about the welfare of the team and its success. Look out for the team as if its success is defined by your actions each day. Look for ways to make the team and its leader look good.

Example

Mary is a project member. She is always looking for opportunities to help her team and team leader look good and be successful. Here are some examples of actions that Mary has taken:

- Created a list of Power Skills like those discussed in this chapter that serve as reminders of the practices that can help promote team success. Working with her project manager, she then meets with the team to establish a set of shared values for the team to adopt.
- Often volunteers for action items that need an owner.
- Frequently volunteers to participate in work meetings; and when she doesn't volunteer, she often is asked to join because of the inspiring and productive value that she adds to these meetings.
- Whenever necessary, works overtime to protect a commitment she has made or to help ensure the success of another area of the project.
- Sometimes represents the project manager in meetings that the project manager is unable to attend.
- Often serves as a sounding board for ideas, problems, and solutions for other team members as well as the project manager.

Discussion

Based on Mary's many actions, she clearly promotes team success and views a primary part of her job is serving her team and team leader. With a team made up of folks like Mary, it's hard to imagine that team will be anything but successful.

Question

I feel that I spend more time than most looking out for the team. But I don't feel that I get the recognition for doing so. Should I pull back some?

Answer

I wouldn't pull back. Keep doing what you are doing. Your positive teamsmanship is likely being noticed. Over time, you will see benefits coming your way because of your contributions. You may be an inspiration to others and not know it. Continue to be who you choose to be. Long term, you are steadfastly making yourself especially valuable to the organization.

Identify a Set of Shared Values

Across this chapter and the last chapter, we have just discussed 15 Power Skills that every team leader desires their members to practice. As you may have already recognized, many of these tenets also will support and encourage the building of relationships—essential for a great team.

Project members who are diligent in demonstrating these Power Skills will serve as outstanding role models for other members. There's nothing better than an example to inspire and spur the members of a team to be great.

As Mary demonstrated in the last Power Skill description, *promote team success*, this list could be a great starting point for team discussion as each tenet is described and examples shared to reinforce the benefit to each member and the team. Of course, other tenets can be added and discussed. I cannot overstate the importance of a team embracing a set of core values—shared values—that can serve to bond and strengthen the members along their journey. Each team member receives a one-page list of Power Skills to day-to-day reference.

If you are relatively inexperienced as a team member, this list of Power Skills may appear daunting. But to your team leaders, it represents what they strive for when recruiting and coaching. You have the ability to shape your behavior and, therefore, your effectiveness to be and remain a valued team member.

Almost all project members want to perform well and to support the success of the team. They want to mimic behavior that will help the team and, in the process, make them look good as well. If you are a project manager or other leader, don't overlook your personal duty to set a consistent example for your team members.

More Q&As

Question

Whose job is it to teach these behaviors and actions that have been discussed in this chapter to project members? Is it really the project manager as you stated earlier in the chapter? Or is it the direct managers of the project members? Or other?

Answer

Managers are the first line of defense to ensure that their employees are being properly trained and developed so that they can reach their potential in the organization or company. However, a project team can be made up of members that report to many different managers. These members may never have been trained as a cohesive unit.

If a project manager assembles a team that does not already know and practice these Power Skills discussed in the last two chapters, then the project manager is responsible for ensuring that his or her team is properly trained and then nurtured throughout the project's duration. So, while the managers have the responsibility for their employees being sufficiently trained, once the project manager comes into the picture, the project manager is accountable for whatever needs to happen to help ensure the business success of the project.

Question

It seems to me that some of the fundamental Power Skills in the last chapter would be great additions to the shared values list described in this chapter. Your view on this?

Answer

Yes, if a team is brainstorming the Power Skills to populate the shared values list that they plan to adopt, it's possible that a few of the foundational Power Skills could be added. Two examples are *embrace integrity in all that you do* and *treat others as you would like to be treated.* However, I intentionally did not want to duplicate Power Skills across the chapters of the book. In the rare cases where I did, the duplicated Power Skill was presented in a different context. You are free to create the shared values list that is most suited for your team.

Question

This chapter identifies and discusses 15 key Power Skills that every leader would like to see in each of their team members. What is so special about identifying 15? Why not 10 or 20?

Answer

Over the years, I have worked with many hundreds of companies—and many more projects and teams. Over time, I have gravitated to these 15 Power Skills as a baseline for the most important behaviors of team members. Of course, I could easily add more, but I don't feel good taking away any of these 15. I view that these 15 tenets—shared values—are fundamental in defining the behaviors that make a team member valuable. However, having said that, the best list is not what I select, it's what the team feels best defines the values from which they will benefit.

List of Power Skills for a Team

Here is a summary list of the 15 Power Skills for a team that we have just discussed. These skills are key behaviors and actions that every team leader would like to see in each of their team members.

Printable Copy

You can obtain a printable copy of the summary list by visiting my website at:

nealwhittengroup.com/powerskills/

Take Accountability for Your Responsibilities

1. *Be truthful.* Be honest and timely when revealing your progress and issues. When you make a mistake, admit to it, and take accountability.
2. *Be reliable.* Meet your commitments. Always do what you say you are going to do and when you said you would do it.
3. *Demonstrate personal initiative.* Practice self-reliance when appropriate. Require minimal leadership. Make things happen.
4. *Ask for help.* Asking for help is a sign of strength, not weakness. Doing so can not only increase your personal value but can be a big benefit to your team.
5. *Practice being proactive.* Make it a standard practice to think one or more steps ahead.
6. *Focus on solutions.* Do not engage in finger-pointing and the blame game. Be a problem solver.
7. *Practice continuous improvement.* Seek ways to continually improve your skills as well as the processes and procedures that you and your team engage in. Be open and accepting to constructive criticism. Encourage feedback on your performance.

Support the Team by Your Personal Behaviors

8. *Fully participate.* Voluntarily speak up in meetings and get-togethers. Be forthcoming to both ask and answer questions.
9. *Share knowledge.* Knowledge is power; the best performers give it away.
10. *Maintain a positive attitude.* Adopt a can-do spirit. Place a constructive view on issues—seek out the sun during cloudy and stormy moments. Don't take or make things personal.
11. *Be willing to compromise.* Compromising on an issue is often required to resolve it. Moreover, compromising can spread goodwill and strengthen relationships.
12. *Support the ideas of others.* Be willing to listen to and be open to the ideas of others.
13. *Give praise to others.* Recognize the contributions of others and give credit where it is due.

14. *Advocate a sense of humor.* Your job is serious business but don't overlook the value of humor to lighten your load. Be willing to laugh at yourself and some of the situations you will find yourself in. If you are not having fun, you are not giving your best.

15. *Promote team success.* Look for ways to make the team and its leader look good. Look out for the team as if its success is defined by your actions each day.

SECTION 3

Power Skills for Interacting With Your Leaders

Your leaders want you to know—need you to know—the behaviors they consistently expect from you. Just because you have a leadership role or aspire for a leadership role doesn't mean you are living up to the expectations of your leaders.

We are going to discuss important behaviors—Power Skills—that your leaders expect from you. By leader, I am talking about your immediate leader who could be a team leader, project manager, or your boss. But I am also talking about any leaders within your leadership chain of command. However, for most readers, I suggest you focus on your immediate boss as you read through these Power Skills.

Each of the 17 Power Skills will be presented and discussed in three segments. The first segment describes the behavior. The next segment offers an example to show the behavior being applied or a missed opportunity. And the last segment further discusses various aspects of the Power Skill being introduced.

I have divided the Power Skills into three categories to enhance their understanding and benefit:

- Communicate with your leaders
- Take ownership of your performance
- Build a reputation.

Again, the Power Skills are listed in no particular order within a category.

One more point. The more you understand what is expected of you from your leader, the more you will likely focus on honing those skills, improving your performance, and in the process, helping your leader look good, which helps you look good. Talk about a win–win! So, if you have an interest in enhancing your image, effectiveness, and career—and who doesn't—let's get to the first Power Skill.

CHAPTER 8

Communicate With Your Leaders

This category reveals the first 8 of the 17 Power Skills for interacting with your leaders:

1. Make it brief
2. Promote dialog
3. Don't take it personally
4. Keep your leaders informed
5. Offer professional criticism
6. Offer praise
7. Wear one face
8. Solicit feedback on your performance.

1.   Make It Brief

When you are speaking with your peers you can speak in paragraphs. When you are speaking with your immediate boss, reduce the paragraphs to sentences. But the higher up the leadership food chain you communicate, learn to shorten the sentences—even approaching sound bites. Your leaders don't have the time for the unabridged version. If they need to know more, they will ask. They respect you more when you can net your messages, so they can obtain the necessary information in the minimal amount of time.

Why are so many people too verbose and tend to speak in paragraphs when speaking to their higher management? A big reason is that we want the higher-level management to know that we are knowledgeable and qualified. We see a meeting with higher-ups to be an opportunity to impress them; maybe even reinforce to them that we are valuable and are a great investment for the company. Well, they already know you are capable and worthy, or you would not be in your position.

Example

Donna is in a leadership position and has some information she believes she should share with her boss, Raul. Donna is walking down the hallway to Raul's office. Raul looks up from his desk and sees Donna headed his way. Donna has earned a reputation of making any conversation with her a lengthy and tedious event. Raul immediately cringes and hopes that Donna is coming this way to see someone else. No such luck.

Donna walks in and begins dumping information on Raul. A minute into the discussion, Raul asks Donna if she will summarize the information in a minute or less; that he has some other items that require his attention. Donna acknowledges and continues for several more minutes. Finally, Raul believes he has ample information and tells Donna that he is preparing for a meeting and must get back to his task. He thanks Donna for her information.

Losing Respect

Had Donna encountered the same situation with a much higher-level manager, that manager likely would have been abrupt and forced the conversation to two minutes or less. Although Donna's boss must take some responsibility for not being more proactive in counseling Donna on this weakness, Donna will continue to lose respect because of her inability to be brief when being brief is called for. We all know a *Donna* in our organizations. Make sure it's not you.

Question

You say to make it brief, but I am concerned that my leaders will not understand the full magnitude of what I say. Most of them are not as technical or knowledgeable as I am, nor do I expect them to be. What do you say about that?

Answer

You need to learn to *read your audience*. People send signals when they've *got it*. Learn to recognize those signals, then move on. Use your best judgment. You may be doing just fine. If in doubt, ask your leaders for feedback.

2.   Promote Dialogue

Don't be a *yes* employee or a silent employee. Don't just take notes, nod, and leave your boss' office. Listen thoughtfully, ask good questions, and raise concerns—if any. Your leaders need your response, your ideas, and your participation.

Example

Ann is called into Miguel's office, her manager. Miguel has an assignment to give her. He had not thought out the assignment very well but expects Ann to ask questions and overall get a good grasp on what she needs to do. Ann knows that Miguel's assignments are often half baked, and it's up to her to help him articulate what she needs to know so she can go off and do the right job.

Ann carries a small *cheat sheet* for these moments to help her get the information she needs. Here's a look at the sample questions on that cheat sheet:

- What, specifically, is the assignment?
- How important is this assignment? What's at stake?
- What is the priority of this assignment versus all my other duties I am currently working?
- Will I need to delay work on other assignments? If so, who should be informed?
- How much time do I have to complete the assignment?
- Where can I go for help if I need it?
- Who else, if anyone, should I work with?
- Are there any limitations or restrictions to moving forward?

- What is the communications path to be used if I have more questions for Miguel?
- What is the communications path for Miguel if he has more information to provide me?
- How often should progress updates be provided? And to whom?
- (of course, more questions can be added here)

Notice what is happening. Ann knows that Miguel doesn't assign work to her that has always been well thought out—but what manager does the first time the work is presented? Ann realizes that it's her job to seek out the information she requires so she can do the best job she can.

Role Model

Miguel knows about Ann's cheat sheet and has asked her to work with some of Miguel's other staff in helping them maturely take on new assignments. Miguel sees Ann as a role model in demonstrating how best to promote dialogue between an employee and her manager.

Question

When my leaders have given me direction, I don't feel I have the latitude to question their marching orders. Do you?

Answer

If the direction is unclear, contradictory, incomplete, or misleading—to name a few—you must professionally speak up to ensure that the proper action results. If you owned the company, would you want your employees to blindly follow your directions—especially if they are confused or need more information? Speaking up—with a tone of respect, of course—does not have to be interpreted as insubordination. It should come across as the opposite: Showing that you care about your job and doing the right thing.

3.   Don't Take It Personally

Don't take all your leader's actions or inactions personally. Be generous with giving them the benefit of the doubt. Cut them some slack as you would hope others would for you. Your leaders may not handle stress any better than anyone else.

Example

Let's look at some examples of behaviors that even the best leaders may occasionally digress to. Let's focus on your immediate manager:

- Doesn't return a call or text within a reasonable time
- Provides you destructive criticism—meaning there is no real value for you to learn and grow
- Provides you constructive criticism but in a destructive tone
- Demonstrates being impatient even though you cannot move on an issue any faster
- Is argumentative rather than rationally discussing an issue
- Appears to not appreciate the big and little things that you do
- Assigns you a task that has not been well thought out.

Promote Understanding

If your boss occasionally—and *occasionally* is the operable word here— demonstrates this behavior, then here's where you want to cut him or her some slack. There will be times when your leaders may occasionally be abrupt, impatient, argumentative, and unappreciative—simply not thinking clearly or effectively. After all, you may have your mood swings from time to time as well.

When your boss gets this way, work with him or her and do your best to help them through this. After the dust settles, hopefully, they will appreciate your great attitude and tell you so. Maybe you will even inspire them to do better themselves.

Question

Where do I draw the line between reasonable behavior and abusive behavior?

Answer

There are so many scenarios that it's difficult to give a general answer. My experience is that you will know the difference when it occurs.

If the uncomfortable behavior exhibited by a leader is an exception from that leader's typical behavior, then in most cases it may be best to let it be. If the behavior is followed by an apology, then, again, chalk it up to the leader having a bad day.

If the unsettling behavior is frequent or personally crosses a line, then you may need to deal with the issue. We all have different thresholds when it comes to taking things personally. What may not be a big deal to me could be unacceptable to you. Play this one carefully. Better to err on the side of cutting too much slack than not enough.

If the situation is a legal or ethical issue, then immediately distance yourself. You should also consider alerting your legal team, human resource department, or other proper authority, depending on the specifics of the issue.

4. Keep Your Leaders Informed

Keep your leaders informed of important news. Don't work in a vacuum. Avoid surprises. However, this doesn't mean you should tell your boss about every problem that comes your way. In fact, don't reveal most problems to your boss. If you did, your boss would cringe every time he or she sees it's you on the phone or at their office door or in an e-mail/text message that just arrived.

You are paid to solve problems. Your boss gains no value in knowing all the problems that you face each day and how each was solved. Therefore, be selective and only share those problems that you feel your boss should know about or that you want your boss to know about. And be discreet in how you share bad news with your boss.

Example

Let's look at an example about sharing news with your boss discreetly. You are a project manager. You have a meeting with your boss at 8:00 a.m. the next day. You arrive to work at 7:30 a.m. and discover a very serious problem on your project. At 8:00 a.m., you walk into your boss' office, and his boss is also sitting there. What do you do? Do you share the bad news with your boss in front of his boss?

No! Unless there is an unusually great relationship between all three of you, do not share this news with both managers at the same time. Instead, ask your boss if you could see him for a moment outside the office. Then share the bad news. Your boss won't like the bad news; however, you share it, but he later will appreciate the discreet way you shared the news. Now it's up to your boss whether this news will immediately be shared with his boss.

If you share the bad news with both managers, your manager could look bad to his boss. For example, his boss may be wondering how such a bad situation with your project could occur without your boss being aware before now. You do not want your boss to look bad if it can reasonably be avoided.

Status Reports

You must decide what information your boss needs to know from day to day and week to week. Of course, you want to avoid your boss being surprised with hearing important news about your assignments and projects from a source other than you. You also may choose to inform your boss of information that she may not require, but because it places you in a favorable light, it is in your best interest that she knows.

I recommend you provide a one-sheet status report to your boss each week or a two-sheet status report each month—especially if your boss doesn't require it. In addition to using the status reports for their communication value, your boss will use these reports as reference when it's time to evaluate your performance.

Content of Status Reports

For example, a weekly status report should show:

1. Your noteworthy accomplishments from the past week
2. Your key plans for next week
3. Top three issues being worked
4. 30-day outlook
5. Items that toot your own horn, if any

6. Other information that can be of interest to your boss such as you will be inaccessible in a class or on vacation for x days next week.

5.   Offer Professional Criticism

If your work-related views run counter to your leaders', then constructively and discreetly share those views. Your value increases when your interest, honesty, and passion are apparent.

Example

Ashley is a project manager who works for Conner. Conner occasionally attends Ashley's routine project tracking meetings. When he does, he has a bad habit of taking them off on a tangent and meaningful progress often comes to a halt. Of course, this situation harms Ashley and the project, but it also places Conner in an unfavorable light with all those folks attending the meeting.

After today's meeting, Ashley decided to stop by and have a private discussion with Conner about these tangents. Ashley knows that Conner means well. She also believes that it's her job to help her boss look good.

Conner was open-minded about Ashley's constructive criticism and was glad that someone told him because, otherwise, he would never have realized his negative impact in those meetings. He just assumed that he was having a positive impact. He knew that Ashley is looking out for her project—and she should—but he also knew by the manner she shared this information, that she was also looking out for him. He couldn't wait for his next opportunity in her project tracking meetings to show that he has rehabilitated himself and that he truly has Ashley's project's best interest in mind.

Be Selective

By the way, you want to be selective in offering professional criticism to your boss, just as your boss should be selective in how often and when you receive professional criticism. As the saying goes, *don't make a mountain out of a molehill*. However, in many cases, offering professional criticism will result in a win–win for both you and your boss.

6.   Offer Praise

When you observe noteworthy ideas, actions, or deeds by your leaders, show that you appreciate their behavior. Do not focus only on criticism—as constructive as it may be.

We all like to receive praise, especially from someone in a powerful position such as our boss or someone higher up. It's interesting that we can easily feel slighted when we don't receive praise, yet we often don't feel any duty to offer praise to our boss or others. Your boss and other leaders are human and appreciate the praise as much as anyone else.

Examples

Here are some examples of behaviors and actions from your boss that may be opportunities for you to show your appreciation and give praise.
Your boss:

- Orders pizza for your team working late one evening
- Approves your request to travel to a professional conference where you can update your knowledge and skills
- Gives you a salary increase
- Creates that special assignment that you were hoping for
- Praises you in front of others for some noteworthy achievement
- Gives you time off for many of those extra hours you worked
- Gives you cash or a gift certificate to a fun place for you and a guest
- Allows you to leave work early on special occasions
- Regularly coaches you so you can learn and grow more rapidly
- Supports your independence and is there for you when you might occasionally fall
- Makes you available to transfer to another department to pursue a special interest
- Covers your back.

Investment in You

There are many opportunities to praise your boss and other leaders around you. The more you raise your awareness of all that your boss has done or continually does, the more likely you will take less of it for granted and appreciate that which you have.

Just as we discussed in offering professional criticism, when you offer praise to your boss, it shows your interest and passion in helping your boss look good and helping to contribute to a healthier work environment. Taking great care of your boss is also an investment in taking care of you.

7.   Wear One Face

Don't be one person when your leaders are around and someone different the rest of the time. Choose the same face regardless of the audience.

Example

A client calls me with a problem and asks if I could help in solving his dilemma. Here's the situation. The client, Howard, is the CIO of an organization of 25 managers. He meets with his group of managers each week for two hours. During that time, they discuss new problems and solutions to those problems.

A typical occurrence is that he will ask the managers for their ideas in solving a particular problem—a problem that they had the past week to reflect upon. It is common for Howard to get little or no ideas from the group. When he does get an idea, it is usually from two or three of the most vocal managers. Otherwise, the meeting room is deafeningly quiet.

When this happens, Howard will advance a solution and bounce that idea out across the managers. Again, mostly the group is quiet. Howard then may say, *Well, I will view you being quiet to mean that you don't have a better idea and that the idea I promoted is acceptable. That being the case, let's adopt my solution and move on to discuss the next issue.*

Howard confides in me that he has discovered that many of these managers, once outside the meeting, attack his ideas and mock him and his ideas as having little to no value. They chatter among themselves that they are surprised that Howard is so naive as to think that these ideas are good and will work. Of course, Howard is frustrated to have so many immature and two-faced managers on his team.

I then conducted training for Howard and his managers to help raise their professional maturity. During the training, I brought up the instance where many managers are showing two faces: one in meetings and the other face away from meetings. I told them how professionals carry the same face all the time. I told them that if they worked for me and I asked them for their ideas to solve problems, but they had none—and I asked for their support in ideas that I had advanced—because no one else had any ideas—and they left me with the impression that my ideas—my direction—were acceptable, but then they undermined my actions once they are outside the meeting—*I WOULD FIRE THEM!*

I expect my managers to be professionally mature—to be teachers to others of how to professionally behave—not to be leading the *immaturity* of the organization. Upon hearing this, one manager asked, *You would give us one chance before firing us, wouldn't you?* I said, *Yes, I would and you're getting that chance right now in this training class.*

Your Authentic Self

By the way, when you always wear one face, you become your authentic self. You become more predictable, constant, and respected with those who work with and around you. You no longer must work at maintaining two or more faces.

Question

By *wear one face*, do you mean do not talk destructively behind your leaders' backs?

Answer

For starters, yes. But I mean much more. I want you to include always projecting a positive attitude about all you do and your relationships with others. Wearing two or more faces not only undermines the best interests of your leaders and the organization, but it also damages your credibility.

8.   Solicit Feedback on Your Performance

Ask for constructive criticism as well as praise based on your actions and behavior. Make it easy—be a willing student—for your leaders to work with you and professionally *shape* you in becoming a more effective leader.

Example

I was in management for over 10 years at a large company. I was often looking for techniques to help my employees grow more quickly and to increase communications between them and me. I put the word out across my organization that they could come visit me at any time and request— on the spot—an evaluation rating of their performance from me. It would be based on my observations of them from meetings, one-on-ones, and other events that they were part of. The on-the-spot performance rating was not binding because my immediate assessment would not have had the benefit of me first doing due-diligence related to their performance. The rating also was not binding because most of the employees did not work directly for me—they worked for managers that reported into me.

After making this offer, I braced myself for an onslaught of employee visits to my office. If I were in an organization that made this offer, I certainly would play. What percentage of my employees do you think took me up on this offer? Ninety-five percent? Fifty percent? Five percent?

About five percent. I just knew at least 50 percent would partake. I learned that most folks really don't want to attract attention to themselves. They don't want to hear news about them if it might not all be positive.

But I also saw that some of the folks with the most interest in performing at their best and growing at a healthy clip did care about the offer. One gentleman, Logan, stopped by and asked for an instant evaluation. I told him it would not be so good. I said that he was one of my senior people and I expect a lot from him. In the past month, I had attended two of his meetings. They were poorly run, had no firm agendas, the meetings continued to drift off topics and didn't appear to achieve the perceived objectives, no minutes of topics resolved were put out afterwards, and more.

The next month, Logan stopped by my office again and asked for an instant evaluation. This time it was glowing. I told him that I had attended three of his meetings since we last talked and they were run great. I told him that I had since used him as a role model in how to run a good meeting and had mentioned him to several other members of the organization.

Bottom Line

Your leaders want you to care about your performance and contributions. When you show interest in your development, they get more interested in you.

CHAPTER 9

Take Ownership of Your Performance

This category reveals the next four of the Power Skills for interacting with your leaders:

9. Don't dump and run
10. Bring solutions with problems
11. Close issues
12. Meet commitments.

9. Don't Dump and Run

When you have an idea for an improvement, don't transfer that idea to your leader and then wash your hands of it. Be willing to be its champion and become part of the solution. Your leaders have neither the duty nor the bandwidth to personally take on and work every good idea to closure.

Example

Dave is a project manager. He works in an organization where the project management methodology has weakly been defined and is marginally encouraged and supported. Dave sees the value to the business in practicing good project management practices. Consequently, he approaches his manager, Jen, and offers the following set of suggestions:

- Identify a manager to champion the adoption and continuous improvement of project management methodologies across the organization

- Identify a nonmanager—that reports to the champion manager—to provide the leadership in creating and rolling out a plan that will accomplish this mission
- Part of the plan can be creating a board of project managers who contribute to the development, review, approval, and implementation of the project management methodology
- Part of the plan can also include piloting project management improvements on various projects to measure their usefulness
- Part of the plan can also include publicly recognizing those project managers whose projects excel, in part, because of their adoption of good project management practices.

Dave is excited about his idea and considers himself a *mover and a shaker* in the organization for his thought leadership. Dave's boss, Jen, likes his ideas here and believes that they would benefit the overall organization. But Jen often sees Dave as an idea person and rarely an action person. Jen asks Dave if he would like to lead the charge on this idea and, if he does, she would take on the champion manager role. Otherwise, she says, she would not have the time to invest in working with someone new to his ideas.

Unfortunately, Dave tells Jen that he had no intention implementing anything; he just wanted to inform management that they should seriously consider advancing the state of project management in the organization.

Nonmanagers Also Have a Duty

Herein lies a common problem in most organizations: Nonmanagers—no matter how senior—often believe that it is up to management to continuously improve an organization. Many nonmanagers don't see that that is also their job.

This reminds me of an article I read that stated why the project management profession is not growing faster around the world. It said the problem was senior management because they don't bring project management concepts to their organizations and nurture the implementation of these concepts.

In my opinion, this was a terribly misinformed article. I believe the biggest part of the problem lies not with senior managers but with project managers themselves. After all, project managers are professionals. They know their craft and its benefits better than anyone, including senior management. In my view, project managers should be the ones championing the adoption and continuous improvement of project management best practices. Project managers should be leading the charge by piloting new ideas and ensuring ongoing improvement. Let's not be so quick to blame others—senior management in this case—let's own the issue and take actions that advance the project management profession.

My assertions here apply to all professions. Take charge and advance your profession. Don't wait for management to act or tell you to act. This is what true professionals do.

Words Don't Make Companies Successful; Actions Do

Going back to the theme of this Power Skill, *don't dump and run*, your leaders want and need your ideas, but they also expect your hands to get dirty from time to time. Words don't make companies successful; actions do.

Question

I often have ideas that I believe are worthy to share with my management, but I just don't have but a fraction of the time that would be required to champion the ideas myself. In this case, do you suggest I keep these ideas to myself?

Answer

Not at all. Obviously, there will be times when the person with the idea cannot find the time to implement the idea. Informing your manager may be enough for your manager to find an owner to take the idea to its completion. The issue here is that employees need to learn to be more involved in shaping an organization; don't sit back and wait for management to provide all the direction or do all the work.

Look around your organization and count the people who stand out as not just idea people but also people who have earned the reputation for turning ideas into practice. In most organizations, this is a small minority. That's sad to me. Even if you don't have the time to advance your idea, perhaps you have some time to contribute as a member of the team who champions the idea. As I said earlier, *Words don't make companies successful; actions do.*

10.   Bring Solutions With Problems

When you are faced with a problem and need help, articulate both the solution and the specific help required. Tell your leaders exactly what you need from them, such as funding, letter of support, escalation support, lifting the freeze on hiring, or approval of a new tool. You are far more likely to obtain their support when you have a solution in hand, and they know precisely what is expected from them to help you carry out the solution.

Example

Barbara is a test team leader on a new development project. After the development team has completed their duties, Barbara's team requires 10 weeks to test the product before it can be placed into a production environment and go live. As the development work progresses, their delivery date to the test team looks like it will slip at least a week or two. Barbara is concerned because her team cannot miss the go-live date because the client has so much riding on that date being met. Making matters worse, there is little buffer in her test schedules.

Barbara has already logged her concerns with the project manager, development team, and senior stakeholders, but she has an idea. She discusses the idea with her manager and with the project manager and they both support her moving forward with the idea.

Barbara meets with the project sponsor, Jose—a senior-level manager who owns and funds the project. She defines a solution to Jose and then states exactly what she needs from him. Barbara tells Jose that she needs $50,000. She will use $30,000 to purchase an automated test tool and the remaining $20,000 to fund contractors converting her current test suite to a set of automated test cases that can mostly be run without human intervention. Barbara tells Jose that if she has this new tool, she believes that she can start the testing as much as two to three weeks late and still finish on the original go-live date because she will be able to test 24/7.

As you can imagine, Barbara receives the $50,000. She also receives the admiration of her peers and the project sponsor. She articulated a solution to a serious problem and clearly stated what she needed her project sponsor to do—and he did. Notice that Barbara was not focused on attacking the development team for potentially delaying their delivery to her, but instead was focused on solutions. Leaders don't blame other people; they're too busy solving problems.

Project Sponsor's Thinking at the End of Another Full Day

As a sidebar, consider what was going through Jose's mind as he was heading home from work at the end of that day. He was thinking, *Boy! Another busy, busy day! It seems all I do these days is go from meeting to meeting. It's hard for me to always see where I'm adding value—making a difference. Oh yeah!! I met today with this test team leader, Barbara. She was very clear on how I could help her solve a problem. I approved the release of $50,000 to her and because so, I played a key role in saving a project's go-live date. You know, I did make a difference today. And about Barbara—I'm keeping an eye on her. She seems to know how to take charge, solve problems, and get us working together.*

Question

When you say, *bring solutions with problems,* do you mean we should come with multiple solutions for a single problem?

Answer

It's usually a good idea to have more than one solution to offer; however, my style, in most cases, is to offer one solution but have one or more tucked away in case I need to fall back on them. I generally believe it is not a good idea to offer up many solutions and have your leaders choose. This smacks of transferring responsibility to them. Take a position. That's what you are paid to do. Tell your leaders what you want them to know. If they are not satisfied, they will let you know.

Question

As a leader, if a member comes to me with a problem and that member is uncertain on where to go from here, should I declare the solution for expediency and move on?

Answer

In most cases, no. Ask her questions to lead her to think for herself and propose a solution herself. This style of coaching will help her self-esteem and prepare her to take on bigger issues. If time is of the essence, then you can be a bit more aggressive in taking the lead in resolving the issue. But turn the experience into a teachable moment whenever you can.

Question

As a leader, if I am uncertain about the best solution to a problem I have, is it okay to ask the opinions of others or should I set a self-reliant example and solve the issue on my own?

Answer

The best leaders frequently include others while on the journey to solving an issue. Doing so can yield a better solution and the inclusion of others helps to build relationships.

11. Close Issues

Don't allow issues to linger or drift. Close them with the urgency that they deserve. Your leaders are watching you. They can see who is closing issues versus who is allowing issues to drift and pile up. They can see who is reliable and who tends to be all talk.

Example

Fareed is one of many leaders in the organization. There are many projects going on and too little time to work them. Fareed has been in the organization for several years. He is smart, knowledgeable, and knows what's going on. He is usually the first person to volunteer to go off and work problems. Of course, this is a relief at the senior levels because every organization wants a go-to person who can take on and solve problems.

Unfortunately, Fareed has shown—over time—that he does not often follow through and close the issues on a timely basis and sometimes they never close. It has gotten to a point where no one wants to give a problem to Fareed—even though he may be qualified to solve it—because of his now-demonstrated poor track record.

Don't Hoard Issues

Most of us know someone like Fareed. In the beginning, he is highly admired for taking on problems that many cannot or will not take on. But—over time—we see the damage that Fareed causes because these problems don't close or take too long to close. Fareed is seen as sloppy and unreliable. He is seen as a talker rather than a doer. Your leaders expect you to not hoard issues but to be trusted to close them reliably and with the appropriate sense of urgency.

12.   Meet Commitments

Meet your commitments, whether day-to-day or long-term. Manage your commitments well. If, at times, commitments may need to be reset, then work with the required parties as soon as possible so that any collateral damage will be minimal. But do not create a pattern of missed commitments where there appears to be no end in sight. The respect you develop across your organization or company will, in large part, be affected by your ability to manage your commitments successfully and maturely.

Example

Harry is a project manager and has made many commitments to his manager, Heather, related to his project. Heather has made her own commitments based on the commitments Harry has made to her. She has made commitments in terms of the project completion date, revenue and profit estimates, availability of people resource rolling off Harry's project and being made available for new projects, just to name a few.

Harry soon discovers that some of his commitments are likely to slip so he does whatever he thinks is reasonable to mitigate the slips but is still unable to ensure the commitments. He discusses the issues with Heather who says that Harry must be able to back up his commitments or change them so that they can be relied upon. Harry then replans and changes his commitments. Heather now must change her commitments that she had made that were based on Harry's original commitments.

Harry's broken commitments make Heather look bad. But at least now Harry's plan has been reworked. Dates have slipped but all this has received the appropriate approval and expectations have been adjusted.

You guessed it: Harry's commitments are again in trouble. In fact, this cycle happens several more times throughout the project. Harry's credibility has been severely damaged, and this has ricocheted onto Heather's credibility.

Don't Miss Reworked Commitments

No one can meet every commitment that they have made, but they should be able to meet most of their commitments. The commitments that slip should be carefully replanned and rarely should they slip again.

Heather rightfully expected Harry to meet his commitments. When he didn't, she rightfully expected him to learn from his mistakes and not repeat them. If you find you are unable to meet a commitment, you should have the serious goal of not missing the reworked commitment.

Question

There are two sections that appear to have some commonality: *close issues* and *meet commitments*. How are these sections different?

Answer

We all make commitments. These commitments typically are tied to activities defined in a project plan. But while working on our committed activities, we often run into problems that can become big enough to formally track. These problems then become *issues* and are turned into *action items*. I could have titled the *close issues* section as *close action items*. And, yes, a person commits to resolve these action items just as they commit to complete activities in a project plan, but the action items tend to be smaller-level commitments compared to the base commitments we have made in a project plan.

CHAPTER 10

Build a Reputation

This category reveals the last five Power Skills for interacting with your leaders:

13. Don't complain
14. Make your leaders look good
15. Support your peers
16. Show you can be trusted
17. Be a role model.

13. Don't Complain

People who habitually complain are a bore and a waste of time and energy to those around them. If you are complaining, you are not solving; you are part of the problem.

For example, if you complain to Person A about something that Person B can fix, then you just wasted your time and that of Person A's. But if you *complain* directly to Person B who can fix the problem, this is not complaining; it's the first step of moving toward a solution.

Example

Marcel and Annabelle are both leaders in the department. They work for Dot. Both Marcel and Annabelle have scheduled 30-minute information-update meetings with Dot. Marcel's meeting takes the full 30 minutes, and Dot notes that Marcel complained about six different things but did not have a constructive solution for any. When Dot would ask Marcel what he thought he should or could do to constructively address each complaint-related area, Marcel dismissed each situation as being mostly not solvable because he has complained about these things for a long time. Marcel has a reputation as a complainer; someone who brings negative energy with him wherever he journeys.

Annabelle's meeting with Dot is over in less than 15 minutes. Annabelle also brings up at least six different problem situations but focuses on what she is doing to mitigate each problem area. She never complains, only informs with the positive actions that she is taking. Annabelle accepts full accountability for her problems and has a reputation for making things happen.

Annabelle or Marcel?

If you were the boss, Dot, who do you see adding the most value to your organization? Right! No brainer! It's Annabelle by a long shot.

By the way, if you get a reputation as a complainer, people may stop listening.

Question

You introduced a character named Marcel who appears to be a habitual complainer. His boss, Dot, is fully aware of his reputation. In this case, isn't Dot at least part of the problem because she isn't coaching him to get past this bad habit?

Answer

Yes, in the beginning, a person's manager is partially accountable for the blemishes of her employees. However, a point can be reached where a manager has done everything reasonable, and the employee, for whatever reason, may choose to be untrainable. Because of the brevity of the example, it is not clear if Marcel is being seriously counseled by Dot. Although your point is well taken that a person's manager does have a duty here, let's not overlook the fact that the employee is still accountable for his behaviors and actions.

14. Make Your Leaders Look Good

Satisfying the needs of your boss—fulfilling, even exceeding, his or her expectations—is your job. That makes your boss look good which makes you look good.

For example, if you are a project manager, you likely have two bosses, your immediate boss, and the project sponsor. If you are a project member, you have your immediate boss, and your project leader. When your boss, project sponsor, or project leader knows that you deliberately are looking out for him or her—covering his or her back at every opportunity, the loyalty of your leader back to you will likely be high.

Your job, simply put, is to make your boss look good. There are people who do not see this as their job, but this thinking can harm their careers.

Example

I have a personal story to share that will drive home this concept of focusing on making your boss look good. Early in my career, I never thought much about the notion of *making your boss look good*. Until, that is, I found myself with a new manager, Dennis. Dennis brought this concept of *making your boss look good* into my work life big time. And I have benefitted ever since. Here's what happened.

I was working in an organization of about 100 people spread across six departments. I was one of the project leaders. We all were working on the same project, an important new software product. (But then, what project isn't important?) All 100 of us were not doing the expected job and were missing commitments and producing subpar quality. The department I reported into was one of the worst in this regard. Because of this, my manager was replaced by a more experienced manager, Dennis, from another location within the company.

Dennis met, one-on-one, with each of his approximately 20 employees to get to know them. I was Dennis' first interview. He made it clear that my job was to make him look good. He wanted me involved in everything related to his department. He wanted deliverables among department members on time. He wanted deliverables from his department to the other departments on time, and from those departments to our department on time. He wanted everything we produce to be quality. When reviews or inspections occurred, he wanted follow-up to make certain that all problems found were corrected. He went on and on. Bottom line, he said, was that he didn't want to have to deal with any problems—that he expected me to deal with them before they got to his office.

When I left his office, my head was spinning with all the responsibility he was piling on me. I wasn't sure that I could live up to this expectation, but I could read an organization chart and he was my boss so I would comply to the best of my ability. This meant I came to work every day focused on what I can do to make my boss look good. For example, if I was walking down the hallway and someone said something derogatory about Dennis (which was rare), I would stop and ask what we can do to fix whatever issue was at hand. I was always positive and focused on solutions. Of course, this made Dennis look good, but it was also making me look good—*really* good.

Within six weeks of Dennis taking over as manager, he was bumped up a level and was now the manager over all 100 people. I was appointed to officially manage his department. Dennis had been grooming me to replace him though I did not know that at the time.

Fast Forward 18 Months

I'm now a manager working in another organization—not at all around Dennis. I am at a large company management conference of 800 managers where 12 managers were receiving a prestigious *Management Excellence Award*. To my surprise, I was one of the 12. The lab director—a senior manager over about 10,000 people—tells the audience of 800 why I technically deserved the award. I'm standing next to him along with my boss. Then my boss added another reason why he thought I deserved the award. He said, *because I made him look so good—far better than he might otherwise look*. Voila! My mind quickly raced to Dennis, a past manager, who taught me the value of making *looking out for your boss* a primary objective.

Focusing More on the People Aspect

Before I met Dennis, my objectives were focused primarily on inanimate things like meeting my commitments in a project plan. After meeting Dennis, my focus was on the human aspect of making my boss and his bosses look good. I still cared about meeting my commitments in project plans but now I was doing it less because it was a commitment to a plan and more because meeting my commitments would help make my bosses look good. I found that me focusing more on the people impact was far more motivating to me.

Question

What if I make my leader look good and he takes all the credit and leaves none for me?

Answer

This could happen but will not in most cases. Most leaders know that their success depends on those around them—that they look good in large part because of the many shoulders they are standing on. It is my experience that most leaders will share the limelight of their successes with those who are deserving. Occasionally, there is the bad apple who is interested only in his or her career or, frankly, may be in the wrong job. Fortunately, this is far less common than the opposite case. Over the long haul, my experience shows that the major contributors to the success of others will be recognized.

15.   Support Your Peers

Be quick to support noteworthy ideas and actions by your co-workers. Choose the collaborative path rather than the competitive or contentious path. Build bridges instead of burning them.

Your leaders want you to work well with others—to be a good team player. Being competitive is fine if your primary competitor is you—always looking to improve your own behaviors and actions but not at the expense of others.

Actions to Support Your Peers

Let's look at some actions you can take to support your peers:

- Be open to new ideas. Hear them out. Be fair with your assessment

- Volunteer to be on committees that promote change
- Volunteer to pilot some of your peers' ideas within your own teams and projects
- Be quick to give credit to others for their good ideas
- Invite one or more peers to work with you on a new and management-visible concept or proposal.

Become a Role Model for Others to Emulate

Work hard to build a reputation of supporting your peers. Not only will this help promote better relationships for you and benefit the organization, but your leaders will also view you as a model for others to emulate.

16.   Show You Can Be Trusted

Don't subscribe to lose lips. Earn the reputation of being a trusted confidant. Don't share private information inappropriately. Show your steadfast support for your boss and the mission.

Examples

Let's look at some tenets to bear in mind to help you gain and retain trust with your leaders:

- Never take an issue over your manager to his manager or higher—unless it is a legal or ethical matter
- Always be honest and upfront with your manager with your views even if they run counter to those of your manager
- Privately, provide your manager constructive criticism in areas where he or she can benefit
- Never disclose to a third party something that your management has revealed to you in confidence
- Never speak negatively to others about your manager unless it nets to a positive portrayal of your boss
- Never undermine your manager either in person or behind his or her back
- Meet your commitments, both small and large.

Re-Earning Trust Can Be Nearly Impossible

Trust is something that must be earned and can take some time to do so. If, while on the journey of earning your leader's trust, you violate that trust in some way, it can be very difficult to re-earn the trust—if you ever can. Therefore, keep this in mind at the start of relationships where trust is a key factor. Don't risk violating the trust of your leaders.

Question

You state, *never take an issue over your manager to his manager or higher—unless it is a legal or ethical matter.* Really? Never?

Answer

As a general rule, when your boss makes a decision, that decision is final providing it is legal and ethical. If you believe that the decision is not in your company's best business interest, you have the duty to inform your boss. But if you cannot convince your boss to your way of thinking, let it go and comply with the decision.

There is another option that many companies support: It's often called the *open door.* Companies with an *open-door* policy tell employees that if they believe that they are being treated unfairly or believe an unjust or improper decision has been made, there is recourse. They can appeal that decision to a higher authority in the company, even if that means going over their boss's head. For example, the appeal may go to a higher boss in the same chain of command, or a special executive designated for such a purpose.

An *open-door* policy is a safety valve for employees to resolve issues professionally and maturely, usually personal ones, which were not satisfactorily resolved using the standard and usual means. Going *open door* over your boss is a highly personal decision—even though your company would say it is not personal nor would it be taken personally. Managers are people, too. And while most managers are mature enough to not take the issue personally; occasionally, a bruised apple slips through. Carefully think through initiating an open door before exercising that path. The *open-door* policy should be used only as a last resort and very infrequently, if ever.

Question

You say to *never take an issue over your manager to his manager or higher,* yet there were many instances in this book where you or the person in an example did escalate an issue to higher management. What am I missing?

Answer

In those examples, the person escalating was not escalating over their manager or over a manager in their line of command, they were escalating over managers that were *not* in their own management chain. If my manager or a manager in my line of command takes a position on an issue, that becomes my position as well. But if managers outside of my management chain take a position, I have no requirement to accept that position if I feel it is not in my job's best interest.

17. Be a Role Model

Without fanfare or recognition, behave in a manner that others can emulate. Promote an organizational culture that supports continual success.

Your leaders are looking for role models that they can implicitly or explicitly showcase to others. True role models are not easy to find in organizations. When a role model is found, that person will likely have a bright future. The business environment can be a tough playground for anyone. But if you strive to take the high road in your behaviors and actions, you will steadfastly see your reputation, respect, and value to your organization grow.

Example

Embracing the list of important Power Skills revealed in this chapter (and, of course, across this book) is an excellent starting point in striving to be a role model. As your experience in your job and working with co-workers increases, the potential to positively influence others as well as the organization will also benefit.

Just know that there will be days when you may want to throw your arms up and say, *This is crazy! What's happening to me is so unfair! I don't want to play anymore!* If you haven't been here, you likely will at least several times in your career. This will pass as you draw strength from many of the Power Skills we have discussed.

Be Someone You Look Up To

The relatively few people around us who are great role models make it look easy. It's not. But you get better at it over time and the payback in helping to promote your career is invaluable. Continuously strive to be someone that you would look up to.

Question

You used the term *role model* while introducing several Power Skills earlier in this chapter, such as *promote dialog* and *support your peers*. Yet now you have revealed a Power Skill centered on being a role model. Did you mean to bring up *role model* so often?

Answer

Yes. I was emphasizing how embracing some Power Skills introduced earlier in the chapter can help set you up as a role model for co-workers—how you can become an inspiration to others.

More Q&As

Question

The list from this section does appear daunting. But isn't this really just common sense?

Answer

No. Common sense can vary widely among cultures. Often the cultures across town can be as diverse as the cultures across the world. Don't assume you know what the accepted culture is from your leaders. If in doubt, approach them to discuss a starter list of these behaviors. Also discuss what may be missing from the list that is especially important to them.

Question

Here again, it seems to me that some of the foundational Power Skills in the first section and some of the Power Skills for a team described in the second section would be great additions to the list of Power Skills presented in this section that are specifically related to interacting with your leaders. Your view on this?

Answer

Yes, this list could be expanded by including some Power Skills from the previous chapters to best create a list that serves your interests. As I said in the previous chapter, I intentionally did not want to duplicate Power Skills across the chapters of the book. In the rare cases where I did, the duplicated Power Skill was intended to be presented in a different context.

Question

Apparently, you believe that leaders can be made?

Answer

Absolutely yes! But even those who are often tagged as *born leaders* need help along the way to fine-tune their craft. Education and experience are both necessary to be the best leader. I like the quote by Vince Lombardi, American football coach:

> *Contrary to the opinion of many people, leaders are not born. Leaders are made, and they are made by effort and hard work.*

List of Power Skills for Interacting With Your Leaders

Here is a summary list of the Power Skills for interacting with your leaders that we have just discussed. Meeting your leaders' expectations can enhance your image, effectiveness, and career.

Printable Copy

You can obtain a printable copy of the summary list by visiting my website at:

nealwhittengroup.com/powerskills/

Communicate With Your Leaders

1. *Make it brief.* Your leaders don't have time for the unabridged version.
2. *Promote dialog.* Your leaders need your response, your ideas, and your participation.
3. *Don't take it personally.* Your leaders may not handle stress any better than anyone else. Cut them some slack as you would hope others would for you.
4. *Keep your leaders informed.* Don't work in a vacuum; keep your leaders informed of important news.
5. *Offer professional criticism.* Your value increases when your interest, honesty, and passion are apparent.
6. *Offer praise.* When you observe noteworthy ideas, actions, or deeds by your leaders, show that you appreciate their behavior.
7. *Wear one face.* Choose the same face regardless of the audience.
8. *Solicit feedback on your performance.* Ask for constructive criticism as well as praise based on your performance.

Take Ownership of Your Performance

9. *Don't dump and run.* Be willing to champion ideas and become part of their solution.
10. *Bring solutions with problems.* Clearly state the support you need from your leaders in terms of solving problems.
11. *Close issues.* Don't allow issues to linger, to drift.
12. *Meet commitments.* Demonstrate that you can be counted on; that you are reliable.

Build a Reputation

13. *Don't complain.* If you are complaining, you are not solving; you are part of the problem.
14. *Make your leaders look good.* Your job is to make your leaders look good, which makes you look good.
15. *Support your peers.* Choose the collaborative path rather than the competitive or contentious path.
16. *Show you can be trusted.* Earn the reputation of being a trusted confidant.
17. *Be a role model.* Without fanfare or recognition, behave in a manner that others can emulate.

APPENDIX A

Questionnaire for Self-Assessing Your Foundational Power Skills

If you have completed *Chapters 1 to 5*, you are ready to take the self-assessment tool here—also called the *Questionnaire*. If you have not yet read these chapters, you can still take the questionnaire; however, it may be a bit less meaningful to you since you will not have been introduced to the foundational Power Skills that the questionnaire will reference.

The purpose of the questionnaire is to gain insight into how proficient you perceive your performance to be in the 24 foundational Power Skills introduced in Chapters 1 to 5. After taking the questionnaire, you will determine your score, and we will discuss what that score might mean to you.

Printable Copy

You can obtain a printable copy of the questionnaire by visiting my website at:

nealwhittengroup.com/powerskills/

Completing the Questionnaire

The questionnaire is comprised of 67 questions. There are six possible answers for each question. The answers have a number associated with them. Circle the number that best represents your answer. When you finish the questionnaire, you will add all the numbers circled and divide by 24. This will yield your score. More on what this score means after you have completed the questionnaire.

You are now ready to take the questionnaire.

Break the rules occasionally

1	As the need presents itself, do you resort to unconventional solutions (that are ethical and legal) in the pursuit of business success?	Always 5	Almost always 4	Sometimes 3	Seldom 2	Never 1	No Comment 0

Never avoid necessary confrontation

2	Do you give problems the sense of urgency and importance they deserve?	Always 1.25	Almost always 1	Sometimes 0.75	Seldom 0.5	Never 0.25	No Comment 0
3	Do you allow others to intimidate you into being less effective than is possible?	Never 1.25	Seldom 1	Sometimes 0.75	Almost always 0.5	Always 0.25	No Comment 0
4	Do you ensure that you make the best business decisions even when others may *not* be happy with those decisions?	Always 1.25	Almost always 1	Sometimes 0.75	Seldom 0.5	Never 0.25	No Comment 0
5	Do you avoid necessary confrontation?	Never 1.25	Seldom 1	Sometimes 0.75	Almost always 0.5	Always 0.25	No Comment 0

Routinely practice boldness and courage to be a consistently effective leader

6	When necessary, do you demonstrate boldness in the performance of your assignments?	Always 2.5	Almost always 2	Sometimes 1.5	Seldom 1	Never 0.5	No Comment 0

| 7 | Do you demonstrate courage when confronted with something that you fear? | Always 2.5 | Almost always 2 | Sometimes 1.5 | Seldom 1 | Never 0.5 | No Comment 0 |

Think for yourself

| 8 | Do you challenge tradition, authority, and the status quo in a professional and mature manner? | Always 2.5 | Almost always 2 | Sometimes 1.5 | Seldom 1 | Never 0.5 | No Comment 0 |
| 9 | Do you routinely question your own behaviors and actions? | Always 2.5 | Almost always 2 | Sometimes 1.5 | Seldom 1 | Never 0.5 | No Comment 0 |

Do not allow what others think about you to be more important than what you think about yourself

| 10 | Do you typically place a higher value on what you think about yourself over what other people think about you? | Always 2.5 | Almost always 2 | Sometimes 1.5 | Seldom 1 | Never 0.5 | No Comment 0 |
| 11 | Is being liked at work a primary objective for you? | Never 2.5 | Seldom 2 | Sometimes 1.5 | Almost always 1 | Always 0.5 | No Comment 0 |

Live in your present moments

| 12 | Do you live in your present moments (versus in the past or the future)? | Always 2.5 | Almost always 2 | Sometimes 1.5 | Seldom 1 | Never 0.5 | No Comment 0 |

| 13 | Are you able to emotionally process any past mistakes or situations so that they do *not* negatively affect your present moments? | Always 2.5 | Almost always 2 | Sometimes 1.5 | Seldom 1 | Never 0.5 | No Comment 0 |

Don't make it personal or take it personally

14	Do you avoid taking things personally and/or making things personal?	Always 1.67	Almost always 1.33	Sometimes 1	Seldom 0.67	Never 0.33	No Comment 0
15	Do you refrain from speaking ill of others (other than privately with that person)?	Always 1.67	Almost always 1.33	Sometimes 1	Seldom 0.67	Never 0.33	No Comment 0
16	Do you do things because they are the right business things to do, not because you or someone else takes things personally?	Always 1.67	Almost always 1.33	Sometimes 1	Seldom 0.67	Never 0.33	No Comment 0

Mind your own business first

| 17 | Do you routinely conduct yourself as if you own the business and the business is defined by your domain of responsibility? | Always 2.5 | Almost always 2 | Sometimes 1.5 | Seldom 1 | Never 0.5 | No Comment 0 |

18	Do you place a higher priority on your own assignments than on looking out for the company? In other words, unless you were directed by your leadership to work on a non-assignment task, do you first steadfastly focus on your own assignments?	Always 2.5	Almost always 2	Sometimes 1.5	Seldom 1	Never 0.5	No Comment 0

Embrace integrity in all that you do

19	Do you volunteer the truth without having to be coaxed or encouraged?	Always 0.71	Almost always 0.57	Sometimes 0.43	Seldom 0.29	Never 0.14	No Comment 0
20	Are you truthful when you make commitments?	Always 0.71	Almost always 0.57	Sometimes 0.43	Seldom 0.29	Never 0.14	No Comment 0
21	Are you truthful about your project progress and problems?	Always 0.71	Almost always 0.57	Sometimes 0.43	Seldom 0.29	Never 0.14	No Comment 0
22	Are you truthful about mistakes you have made that can benefit others knowing about them?	Always 0.71	Almost always 0.57	Sometimes 0.43	Seldom 0.29	Never 0.14	No Comment 0
23	Do you do the right thing?	Always 0.71	Almost always 0.57	Sometimes 0.43	Seldom 0.29	Never 0.14	No Comment 0

24	Do you condemn unethical or illegal behavior?	Always 0.71	Almost always 0.57	Sometimes 0.43	Seldom 0.29	Never 0.14	No Comment 0
25	Do you refrain from lying or distorting the truth?	Always 0.71	Almost always 0.57	Sometimes 0.43	Seldom 0.29	Never 0.14	No Comment 0

Manage daily to your top three priorities

26	At any given moment, can you identify your top three priorities that you need to be working?	Always 1.25	Almost always 1	Sometimes 0.75	Seldom 0.5	Never 0.25	No Comment 0
27	Do you begin each day with a to-do list that identifies your top three priorities for the day?	Always 1.25	Almost always 1	Sometimes 0.75	Seldom 0.5	Never 0.25	No Comment 0
28	Do you focus on your top three priorities most days?	Always 1.25	Almost always 1	Sometimes 0.75	Seldom 0.5	Never 0.25	No Comment 0
29	Do you work off your top three priorities at least weekly and replace them with new priorities?	Always 1.25	Almost always 1	Sometimes 0.75	Seldom 0.5	Never 0.25	No Comment 0

Trust but verify; inspect what you expect

30	Do you require plans, metrics, and checks and balances to ensure that important commitments are planned and trackable?	Always 1.67	Almost always 1.33	Sometimes 1	Seldom 0.67	Never 0.33	No Comment 0

31	Unless a person has appropriately earned your trust, do you typically inspect what you expect from others?	Always 1.67	Almost always 1.33	Sometimes 1	Seldom 0.67	Never 0.33	No Comment 0
32	Do you believe that you are at least partially accountable for the quality and timeliness of deliverables to you from others?	Always 1.67	Almost always 1.33	Sometimes 1	Seldom 0.67	Never 0.33	No Comment 0

Treat others as you would like to be treated

33	Do you treat others the way that you would like them to treat you?	Always 2.5	Almost always 2	Sometimes 1.5	Seldom 1	Never 0.5	No Comment 0
34	When you are faced with negative behavior by a co-worker, do you take the high road and respond in a manner that you would wish the person had originally adopted?	Always 2.5	Almost always 2	Sometimes 1.5	Seldom 1	Never 0.5	No Comment 0

Think like a leader

35	Do you practice that leadership is *not* about the ability of those around you to lead, but about your ability to lead regardless of what is happening around you?	Always 2.5	Almost always 2	Sometimes 1.5	Seldom 1	Never 0.5	No Comment 0

36	Do you practice leadership that sees your role as predominantly serving, developing, and nurturing others rather than focusing on yourself?	Always 2.5	Almost always 2	Sometimes 1.5	Seldom 1	Never 0.5	No Comment 0

Treat all project members equally

37	Do you hold each team on a project just as accountable for its commitments as any other team?	Always 2.5	Almost always 2	Sometimes 1.5	Seldom 1	Never 0.5	No Comment 0
38	Do you give preferential treatment to some project members?	Never 2.5	Seldom 2	Sometimes 1.5	Almost always 1	Always 0.5	No Comment 0

Understand and practice empowerment

39	Do you have a good understanding of what is expected of you in your job?	Always 2.5	Almost always 2	Sometimes 1.5	Seldom 1	Never 0.5	No Comment 0
40	Do you take charge of your job (versus wait for others to direct you)?	Always 2.5	Almost always 2	Sometimes 1.5	Seldom 1	Never 0.5	No Comment 0

Seek out a mentor

41	Do you seek out a mentor when doing so would be most helpful?	Always 5	Almost always 4	Sometimes 3	Seldom 2	Never 1	No Comment 0

Treat your customer as if it matters

42	Do you treat your customer as if the future of your company and your employment rests upon your ability to satisfy your customer on the transaction being performed right now?	Always 2.5	Almost always 2	Sometimes 1.5	Seldom 1	Never 0.5	No Comment 0
43	If you conducted a survey of your customer's satisfaction with your performance, would the survey results give you high marks?	Always 2.5	Almost always 2	Sometimes 1.5	Seldom 1	Never 0.5	No Comment 0

Promote mutual relationships

44	Do you schedule time to network and develop relationships?	Always 1.25	Almost always 1	Sometimes 0.75	Seldom 0.5	Never 0.25	No Comment 0
45	Do you return texts, phone calls, and e-mails efficiently?	Always 1.25	Almost always 1	Sometimes 0.75	Seldom 0.5	Never 0.25	No Comment 0
46	Do you take some action daily that can strengthen a relationship?	Always 1.25	Almost always 1	Sometimes 0.75	Seldom 0.5	Never 0.25	No Comment 0

47	Do you generously give co-workers the recognition they have earned?	Always 1.25	Almost always 1	Sometimes 0.75	Seldom 0.5	Never 0.25	No Comment 0

Evaluate yourself daily

48	Do you believe there is sufficient benefit in evaluating your performance daily?	Always 2.5	Almost always 2	Sometimes 1.5	Seldom 1	Never 0.5	No Comment 0
49	Do you evaluate your performance daily or weekly?	Always 2.5	Almost always 2	Sometimes 1.5	Seldom 1	Never 0.5	No Comment 0

Promote diversity, equity, and inclusivity

50	Do you regularly promote diversity, equity, and inclusion in your team and organization?	Always 1	Almost always 0.8	Sometimes 0.6	Seldom 0.4	Never 0.2	No Comment 0
51	Do you take the time to listen to all team members, not just the vocal ones?	Always 1	Almost always 0.8	Sometimes 0.6	Seldom 0.4	Never 0.2	No Comment 0
52	Do you ensure there is no special treatment for any team members?	Always 1	Almost always 0.8	Sometimes 0.6	Seldom 0.4	Never 0.2	No Comment 0
53	Do you solicit ideas from the entire team for creating a team's core/shared values, so everyone has a role in defining the team's culture?	Always 1	Almost always 0.8	Sometimes 0.6	Seldom 0.4	Never 0.2	No Comment 0

54	Do you implement an open-door policy where diversity, equity, and inclusivity concepts and practices can be discussed?	Always 1	Almost always 0.8	Sometimes 0.6	Seldom 0.4	Never 0.2	No Comment 0

Be a champion for work–life balance

55	Do you habitually put off the important and fun things in your life until later?	Never 1.25	Seldom 1	Sometimes 0.75	Almost always 0.5	Always 0.25	No Comment 0
56	Are you satisfied with your work–life balance?	Always 1.25	Almost always 1	Sometimes 0.75	Seldom 0.5	Never 0.25	No Comment 0
57	Do you believe that the outcome of your day, week, and month is predominately based on the decisions that you have made throughout each day?	Always 1.25	Almost always 1	Sometimes 0.75	Seldom 0.5	Never 0.25	No Comment 0
58	As a rule, do you put yourself first in your life?	Always 1.25	Almost always 1	Sometimes 0.75	Seldom 0.5	Never 0.25	No Comment 0

Have fun in your work

59	Do you look forward to your workday?	Always 1.67	Almost always 1.33	Sometimes 1	Seldom 0.67	Never 0.33	No Comment 0
60	Do you find ways to have fun at work?	Always 1.67	Almost always 1.33	Sometimes 1	Seldom 0.67	Never 0.33	No Comment 0
61	Do you believe that you (versus someone else) are responsible for finding ways to make work fun?	Always 1.67	Almost always 1.33	Sometimes 1	Seldom 0.67	Never 0.33	No Comment 0

Decide who you choose to be

62	Do you define who you choose to be rather than allow others to define it for you?	Always 2.5	Almost always 2	Sometimes 1.5	Seldom 1	Never 0.5	No Comment 0
63	Do you believe that you have substantial control over your own destiny?	Always 2.5	Almost always 2	Sometimes 1.5	Seldom 1	Never 0.5	No Comment 0

Be a good actor

64	Do you successfully manage your external emotions?	Always 1.25	Almost always 1	Sometimes 0.75	Seldom 0.5	Never 0.25	No Comment 0
65	Do you exude self-confidence?	Always 1.25	Almost always 1	Sometimes 0.75	Seldom 0.5	Never 0.25	No Comment 0
66	Do you remain composed under pressure?	Always 1.25	Almost always 1	Sometimes 0.75	Seldom 0.5	Never 0.25	No Comment 0
67	Do you maintain a positive attitude?	Always 1.25	Almost always 1	Sometimes 0.75	Seldom 0.5	Never 0.25	No Comment 0

Assessing Your Score

At this point, you are ready to add all the numbers that you have circled. Divide that number by 24, the number of foundational Power Skills. This will give you a score. Notice that if you answered one or more questions by circling the *0-No comment*, this will negatively affect your score. I am hoping you will take a position on every question.

Here's what the score means:

4.5–5.0: Very impressive—role model caliber

3.8–4.4: Good—with some areas to improve

3.2–3.7: Fair—with many areas to improve

2.6–3.1: Weak—needs to improve

0.0–2.5: Poor—not contributing your fair share.

How Reliable Is Your Score?

Your score is not precise and obviously has some subjectivity since it is self-perception based. However, my experience is that the overall assessment does have value in providing a general range or view of your performance proficiency related to the 24 foundational Power Skills.

Your score is based on the questionnaire treating each of the 24 Power Skills equally. However, in reality, it is not likely that each Power Skill is equally weighted with all others. For example, *think for yourself* will likely be more impactful than *live in your present moments* for most people. Moreover, some Power Skills may have more impact for some folks depending on their vocation or their experience. For example, an experienced person is less likely to require a mentor (*seek out a mentor*).

Your score is also helpful to use as a baseline. You can choose to periodically retake the questionnaire with the goal of improving your overall performance score.

Most importantly, however, the assessment provides a great tool for your own reflection and possibly to discuss with your manager, mentor, peer, or friend. The questions and the resulting assessment values can help you face important issues that must be dealt with as you strive to continuously improve your performance.

To obtain a more objective evaluation of your behaviors and actions, consider having someone who closely works with you take the assessment about you.

Next Step?

After completing the questionnaire, you now have a sense of what Power Skills may need improvement for your performance to improve. Go now (after reviewing the Q and As below) to *Appendix B. Determine Top 3 Power Skills of Importance to You* to continue this performance improvement journey. Or you can move on to the remaining book chapters and circle back to the appendix exercises later.

Question

My score was lower than I expected and what I believe it should be. The reason appears to be the answers that are available to get the highest score on each question. For example, the highest answer score is only possible if you answer *always* or *never*, depending on the question. Both *always* and *never* are absolute and quite rigid, so I mostly answered *almost always* or *almost never* for many of the questions. Comments?

Answer

There are several points I would like to make here:

1. Remember, the scores are not expected to perfectly reflect your performance. They are considered subjective primarily because they are based on your perspective.
2. My experience is that the scores *do* roughly represent your ballpark performance.
3. Whatever score you calculate, it becomes a baseline should you retake the questionnaire. Therefore, if you improve at all, it will still be reflected regardless of the baseline score perfectly representing you.
4. I considered using an answer range of higher granularity so there would be more choices in response to each question. This extra granularity would mostly address your issue with *always* and *almost always*. However, I felt that I was making answering the questions too difficult and in too much detail. Whether I increase the number of answer choices or not, the essence of your answers will still be captured so that the self-assessment will be useful.

Question

Although I agree with most of the foundational Power Skills, I have some reservations about adopting some of them, two examples being *break the rules occasionally* and *never avoid necessary conflict*. Therefore, I disagree with those Power Skills being included in the scoring of the questionnaire. Comments?

Answer

You are free to adopt any or all the Power Skills. In fact, you could delete the questionnaire questions on the Power Skills you choose not to embrace. Then, after you have added all your numerical answers, divide not by 24 (the original number of Power Skills) but by the number of Power Skills that remained after you deleted some. Note, however, if you delete a Power Skill, you must ignore all questionnaire questions related to that Power Skill.

I should add that, as the author of the 24 foundational Power Skills, my experience asserts that all of them are relevant if you want to achieve exceptional performance—that is, be the best you can be. Regardless, I am encouraged that you will benefit from the book. I respect you thinking for yourself.

Question

Under the section *How Reliable Is Your Score?*, you mentioned some reasons why the questionnaire questions cannot be equally weighted. This being the case, do you still assert that this questionnaire is all that useful?

Answer

Without a doubt, I find the questionnaire beneficial! The questions offer you insight into your mastery of the foundational Power Skills. The questionnaire also offers a beneficial exercise leading into deciding your top three Power Skills with which to focus. As I said earlier, you also benefit by creating a baseline score to later compare your progress.

Question

I see great benefits from the questionnaire. Can I make copies and use them with my team?

Answer

Yes. All I ask is that you include the copyright and acknowledge where you got the questionnaire (this book) and the author (me), all of which are already printed on the takeaways on my website.

APPENDIX B

Determine Top 3 Power Skills of Importance to You

The purpose of this exercise instrument is to determine the top three Power Skills with which you need to focus in your quest to achieve exceptional performance.

Notice from the Power Skills table below that the Power Skills for you to improve upon are selected from the 24 foundational Power Skills that were introduced in Chapters 1 to 5. There is space reserved at the end of the table that you can use to optionally add additional Power Skills that we did not discuss but you believe have special importance to you.

Printable Copy

You can obtain a printable copy of the table by visiting my website at:

nealwhittengroup.com/powerskills/

Here's how to use this exercise instrument. For each Power Skill, circle an H (high), M (medium), or L (low) in the *1st Pass* column to designate how important you believe this behavior is to you in helping you improve your performance with the potential goal of achieving exceptional performance. Afterward, count the number of Power Skills that were assigned an *H*. The objective is to end this exercise with your top three selections. If the count of behaviors assigned an *H* is more than three, then repeat the exercise only for those behaviors that were assigned an *H* and circle the appropriate H, M, or L in the *2nd Pass* column.

For example, if the outcome from the first pass was that 10 Power Skills were assigned an *H* then relook at only these 10 Power Skills and decide, relevant to each other, which Power Skills are rated an H, M, or L. If you still have more than three Power Skills assigned an *H* then perform the exercise again using the *3rd Pass* column. Hopefully, you will identify your three most important Power Skills within three passes; if not, continue this exercise until you have your top three behaviors identified.

Before proceeding, I have a tip for you that may help you zero in on your top three Power Skills with which to focus. Look back at the answers you circled for each of the 67 questions in the questionnaire. You can ask yourself the following question for each of the 67 questions and answer by selecting from five possible answers:

Are you satisfied with your score?
5-Very; 4-Satisfied; 3-Somewhat; 2-Hardly; and 1-Not satisfied

This exercise can help you find the Power Skills that you were least satisfied with your mastery. Of course, keep in mind you will be attempting to identify the top three Power Skills to focus on. Not being satisfied with your response doesn't guarantee that Power Skill will be one of the top three to work on but it will garner your attention as a possible candidate to consider.

After you have identified your top three Power Skills, go to *Appendix C. Performance Improvement Plans* and follow the instructions to develop plans that will help you improve your Power Skills in these areas.

Power Skill	1st Pass	2nd Pass	3rd Pass
Break the rules occasionally. Oftentimes, you will find that following conventional rules will not effectively or efficiently solve an issue.	H M L	H M L	H M L
Never avoid necessary confrontation. Always give problems the sense of urgency and importance they deserve.	H M L	H M L	H M L
Routinely practice boldness and courage to be a consistently effective leader. Your behavior drives your success.	H M L	H M L	H M L
Think for yourself. Challenge tradition, authority, and the status quo in a professional and mature manner. Routinely question your own behaviors and actions.	H M L	H M L	H M L

Power Skill	1st Pass	2nd Pass	3rd Pass
Do not allow what others think about you to be more important than what you think about yourself. Listen for helpful snippets but remain in control of you.	H M L	H M L	H M L
Live in your present moments. Don't dwell on yesterday. Admit mistakes, learn from them, apply those lessons going forward … and move on.	H M L	H M L	H M L
Don't make it personal or take it personally. It's all about what's best for business.	H M L	H M L	H M L
Mind your own business first. Behave as if you own the business and your business is defined by your domain of responsibility.	H M L	H M L	H M L
Embrace integrity in all that you do. Listen to your inner voice and treat it as the wise and trusted friend it is.	H M L	H M L	H M L
Manage daily to your top three priorities. They define your value and contributions and, ultimately, your career.	H M L	H M L	H M L
Trust but verify; inspect what you expect. Strive to build trust among project stakeholders, but insist on metrics, checks and balances, and other tools to ensure outcomes are being met.	H M L	H M L	H M L
Treat others as you would like to be treated. You will be remembered and revered for how you made others feel.	H M L	H M L	H M L
Think like a leader. It's not about the ability of those around you to lead; it's about your ability to lead, regardless of what is happening around you.	H M L	H M L	H M L
Treat all project members equally. All project members, regardless of where they come from or to whom they report, must be held accountable for their commitments.	H M L	H M L	H M L
Understand and practice empowerment. Understand your job, take ownership of it, and do whatever is necessary—within legal and ethical parameters—to accomplish it.	H M L	H M L	H M L

(Continues)

(Continued)

Power Skill	1st Pass	2nd Pass	3rd Pass
Seek out a mentor. We can learn far more and far faster when we can draw strength from those who have gone before us.	H M L	H M L	H M L
Treat your customer as if it matters … as if the future of your company and your employment rests upon your ability to satisfy your customer on the transaction being performed right now.	H M L	H M L	H M L
Promote mutual relationships. When your relationships are viewed as strong, more can get done in less time, with less stress, with greater productivity, and you probably like your job more.	H M L	H M L	H M L
Evaluate yourself daily. As professionals, self-assessments of our actions are essential for our continued growth, professional maturity, and effectiveness.	H M L	H M L	H M L
Promote diversity, equity, and inclusivity. Benefits include employees are more engaged, feel more appreciated and respected, and their commitment, trust, and morale increase. However, DEI must be implemented fairly and justly.	H M L	H M L	H M L
Be a champion for work–life balance. Almost everyone wishes they had realized the importance of work–life balance sooner rather than later. Doing so can mean less regrets and a more deliberate life. But whatever your age, you can still seize control and drive toward the balance you most desire.	H M L	H M L	H M L
Have fun in your work. Finding fun in your job is important at so many levels from benefiting your productivity, increasing motivation, reducing stress, making your day go faster, and boosting your career enjoyment.	H M L	H M L	H M L

Power Skill	1st Pass	2nd Pass	3rd Pass
Decide who you choose to be. This book is exposing you to important Power Skills that can change your career and your life. You can cherry pick the Power Skills you choose to embrace or go all out and seriously consider them all when their use can make a difference.	H M L	H M L	H M L
Be a good actor. Continuously work at being the person you choose to be. You first identify a Power Skill to adopt. Then you act on that thought to replace an old behavior with the more desirable behavior.	H M L	H M L	H M L
	H M L	H M L	H M L
	H M L	H M L	H M L
	H M L	H M L	H M L
	H M L	H M L	H M L
	H M L	H M L	H M L

Question

You suggest I identify my top three Power Skills to work. What if I only want to work one or two?

Answer

Totally fine. What's important is that you feel you are making forward progress with your performance improvement. There is no rush. Go with your preferred pace. We all have those moments when we have very limited time to invest. I respect that you are making any time at all.

APPENDIX C

Performance Improvement Plan

Once you have decided the Power Skills you most want to improve, this exercise template can be used to develop a Performance Improvement Plan—one for each of the Power Skills you have chosen to work on. Of course, you could work on more than three Power Skills at the same time; however, better to focus on improving three (or less) Power Skills than to take on many more and be overwhelmed and ultimately ineffective in improving on most or all the selected Power Skills.

There are six areas to be completed for each Performance Improvement Plan:

1. Identify Power Skill to be improved.
2. Recall incident where this Power Skill was weak or missing.
3. Identify the potential or real harm that occurred.
4. Identify the inhibitors that contributed to the weak behavior.
5. Identify a more effective approach utilizing the desired behavior.
6. Identify the benefit that could have resulted from taking a more effective approach.

Printable Copy

I have included a template that you can use to create the Performance Improvement Plan. The template is provided at the end of this appendix. However, you can obtain a printable copy of this template by visiting my website at:

nealwhittengroup.com/powerskills/

You will notice that the Performance Improvement Plan encourages you to examine your current behaviors and consider substituting new behaviors going forward. In other words, looking at the behaviors that you would examine, if the same situations availed themselves tomorrow, would you have learned from your past and behaved more effectively—as your new Performance Improvement Plan suggests? I have found that most people likely know when their behavior is less than optimal. They also have good ideas about what they should have done. The problem comes in when it is time to choose their behavior and they sometimes revert to old habits.

Consider revisiting this exercise template periodically—such as every one to two months. This time period will likely give you sufficient time to practice your top three Power Skills. If, after one to two months, you are not ready to move on to creating plans for new Power Skills, that's okay. As I said earlier, you are not in any race. It's important that you pace to your comfort zone.

Before you begin to develop the Performance Improvement Plans, check out the sample Performance Improvement Plan below that has been completed for your reference. I chose to focus on the Power Skill called, *manage daily to your top three priorities* because I have found this to be one of the most popular Power Skills for readers to focus on.

Sample Performance Improvement Plan

1. **Identify Power Skill to be improved:**
   Manage daily to your top three priorities.
2. **Recall incident where this Power Skill was weak or missing:**
   Upon examining my daily to-do lists with which I began each day last week, it is strikingly apparent that I did not identify my top three priorities to work each day. Moreover, most of each day was also consumed with reacting to interruptions, noise, and minutia that routinely comes my way. As a result, the most important issues and actions frequently did not receive the attention that their importance required.
3. **Identify the potential or real harm that occurred:**
   As a project manager, a recent review of the health of my project revealed that the project's top three problems (priorities) primarily

resulted because they did not receive sufficient care and feeding that they required weeks earlier. As a result, there were unresolved issues causing staffing delays, incomplete and delayed key project documentation, and customer relationship issues.

4. **Identify the inhibitors that contributed to the weak behavior.** The major inhibitor was my lack of knowledge of the importance of managing daily to my top three priorities.

5. **Identify a more effective approach utilizing the desired behavior:** I will create a to-do list at the start of each day. The list will include the top three priorities with which to maximize my attention. I will list on my office whiteboard my top three priorities. This will serve as a conscious reminder to me throughout the day what I view to be my priorities. My goal will be to either resolve or to put a committed plan in place to resolve those items and, within two to three days, remove them from my top three priority list and replace each with a new priority. If I only have a few minutes between meetings to work on my to-do list, I may choose to work on the non-top-three problems. However, whenever I can find 30 minutes or more, I will mostly focus my attention working off my top three priorities.

6. **Identify the benefit that could have resulted from taking a more effective approach:** I expect my effectiveness to improve as I consciously focus on the big-ticket problems that have the most impact on my value and contributions to my project and organization—and ultimately my career. I expect my project to benefit with major issues increasingly receiving the appropriate time and attention they require.

Question

How do I know if I have created a reasonable Performance Improvement Plan?

Answer

It can be helpful if you get an opinion from someone you respect and trust. That could be your boss, a co-worker, a close and honest friend, or someone you view to have mastered the Power Skill you are focusing on, if other than the short list I just mentioned. However, any plan is better than no attempt at a plan. I respect your initiative!

Question

You suggest my manager could be a good source to review my Performance Improvement Plan. Is this really a good idea?

Answer

It could be, but think this through carefully. The upside to exposing the plan to your boss is that your manager likely has relevant experience and skills whereby you could benefit from his or her review. Also, your boss would likely think more highly of you because you are actively working to increase your performance and effectiveness. The downside is that you are exposing weaknesses in your current performance that could then show up in your next performance evaluation and you may get zinged for it. Having said all this, if you have a good working relationship with your boss and feel you won't be harmed by exposing your weaknesses, don't overlook tapping into your boss' skills to aid you.

Performance Improvement Plan Template

1. Identify Power Skill to be improved:

   _____

   _____

   _____

   _____

   _____

2. Recall incident where this Power Skill was weak or missing:

   _____

   _____

   _____

   _____

   _____

   _____

3. Identify the potential or real harm that occurred:

_____

_____

_____

_____

_____

_____

4. Identify the inhibitors that contributed to the weak behavior:

_____

_____

_____

_____

_____

_____

5. Identify a more effective approach utilizing the desired behavior:

_____

_____

_____

_____

_____

_____

6. Identify the benefit that could have resulted from taking a more effective approach:

_____

_____

_____

_____

_____

_____

About the Author

Neal Whitten is a popular speaker, trainer, consultant, mentor, and author in the areas of power skills and leadership, project management, team building, and employee development. He has more than 40 years of front-line experience.

In his 23 years at IBM, Neal held both project leader and management positions. He managed the development of numerous software products, including operating systems, business and telecommunications applications, and special-purpose programs and tools. For three years, he also managed and was responsible for providing independent assessments on dozens of projects for an Assurance group. Neal is president of The Neal Whitten Group, created shortly after leaving IBM in 1993.

Neal is a frequent presenter and keynote speaker at conferences, seminars, workshops, and special events.

He has developed dozens of leadership, project management, and personal development classes and presented to many thousands of people from across hundreds of companies, institutions, and public organizations.

Neal has developed over 20 popular online products (Velociteach .com) available to the public.

Neal is the author of eight books. He has written over 150 articles for professional magazines and was a contributing editor of PMI's PM Network® magazine for over 15 years.

Neal is a member of PMI® and has been a certified Project Management Professional (PMP)® since 1992. You can learn more about Neal by going to his website: www.nealwhittengroup.com.

E-mail: neal@nealwhittengroup.com

Kindly note: Consider bringing the 1-day workshop version of this book to your organization. To learn more, visit nealwhittengroup .com/power-skills-that-lead-to-exceptional-performance/

Index

OTHER TITLES IN THE PORTFOLIO AND PROJECT MANAGEMENT COLLECTION

Timothy J. Kloppenborg, Xavier University and
Kam Jugdev, Athabasca University, Editors

- *When Graduation's Over, Learning Begins* by Roger Forsgren
- *Project Control Methods and Best Practices* by Yakubu Olawale
- *Managing Projects With PMBOK 7* by James W. Marion and Tracey Richardson
- *Shields Up* by Gregory J. Skulmoski
- *Greatness in Construction History* by Sherif Hashem
- *The Inner Building Blocks* by Abhishek Rai
- *Project Profitability* by Reginald Tomas Lee
- *Moving the Needle With Lean OKRs* by Bart den Haak
- *Lean Knowledge Management* by Roger Forsgren
- *The MBA Distilled for Project & Program Professionals* by Bradley D. Clark
- *Project Management for Banks* by Dan Bonner
- *Successfully Achieving Strategy Through Effective Portfolio Management* by Frank R. Parth

Concise and Applied Business Books

The Collection listed above is one of 30 business subject collections that Business Expert Press has grown to make BEP a premiere publisher of print and digital books. Our concise and applied books are for...

- Professionals and Practitioners
- Faculty who adopt our books for courses
- Librarians who know that BEP's Digital Libraries are a unique way to offer students ebooks to download, not restricted with any digital rights management
- Executive Training Course Leaders
- Business Seminar Organizers

Business Expert Press books are for anyone who needs to dig deeper on business ideas, goals, and solutions to everyday problems. Whether one print book, one ebook, or buying a digital library of 110 ebooks, we remain the affordable and smart way to be business smart. For more information, please visit www.businessexpertpress.com, or contact sales@businessexpertpress.com.

Made in the USA
Middletown, DE
10 September 2024

60703344R00126